CW00742483

TO

_____

FROM

_____

DATE

_____

DEVOTIONS TO UPLIFT & ENCOURAGE

busy moms

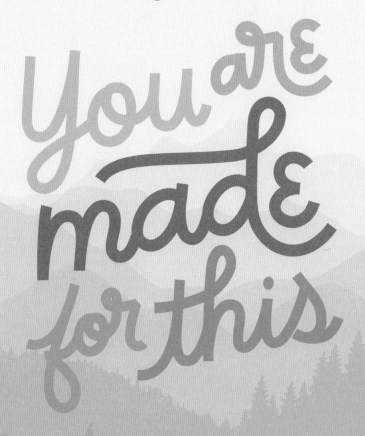

You are
made
for this

MELISSA HORVATH

DaySpring

LIVE YOUR FAITH

You Are Made For This: Devotions to Uplift & Encourage Busy Moms
Copyright © 2024 Melissa Horvath. All rights reserved.
First Edition, March 2024

Published by:

21154 Highway 16 East
Siloam Springs, AR 72761
dayspring.com

All rights reserved. *You Are Made For This: Devotions to Uplift &
Encourage Busy Moms* is under copyright protection. No part of this
book may be used or reproduced in any manner whatsoever without
written permission except in the case of brief quotations embodied in
critical articles and reviews.

Unless otherwise indicated, all Scripture quotations are taken from
the ESV Bible® (The Holy Bible, English Standard Version®) copyright
©2001 by Crossway Bibles, a publishing ministry of Good News
Publishers. Used by permission. All rights reserved.

Scripture quotations marked ERV are taken from the HOLY BIBLE:
EASY-TO-READ VERSION ©2014 by Bible League International. Used
by permission.

Scripture quotations marked GNT are taken from the Good News
Translation in Today's English Version- Second Edition Copyright ©
1992 by American Bible Society. Used by Permission.

Scripture quotations marked NIV are taken from THE HOLY BIBLE,
NEW INTERNATIONAL VERSION®, NIV® Copyright © 1973, 1978, 1984,
2011 by Biblica, Inc.® Used by permission. All rights reserved worldwide.

Written by: Melissa Horvath
Cover Design by: Jessica Wei
Handlettering by: Lauren Purtle

Printed in China
Prime: U2663
ISBN: 979-8-88602-860-7

Contents

Introduction

As moms, we are busy. Each day, we need encouragement. Often, we can think we're going about life on our own—encountering struggles, experiencing highs and lows, and having those days when we just want to hide in the pantry and eat all the chocolate. We do a lot and are responsible for a lot! I'll be the first one to say I'm not perfect and I don't have it all together. But in the little moments, God gently nudged me with thoughts to share with you—whether it be during a heartfelt song at church, a peaceful walk, or even admidst tears in the shower. My hope in sharing these thoughts is to uplift and inspire you on your motherhood journey. I like to say the messages in this book are from Him, through me, to you. I believe God uniquely designed us to fit exactly what our specific children need in a mama. Now we have the *big* responsibility of guiding and loving our children, helping them to know that God is in their corner and for them, always.

But know this, Mama—God is cheering you on along the way! My hope is that this little book will help you for years to come. And you will know that you *can* do this, God *is* for you, and together, You *will* successfully accomplish this up-and-down, roller coaster of a journey called motherhood. I hope you grab a good cup of coffee or tea . . . even break out that ice cream or chocolate from your stash (and if you don't have a stash yet, I highly recommend it!), and let's dive in . . .

Cheers!
Melissa

Into the World

But the angel said to her,
"Do not be afraid, Mary;
you have found favor with God."
LUKE 1:30 NIV

I bet you can remember the first time you saw your child's face. No matter how that came to be, you were chosen from above to be their mama, mom, mommy, mother—how wonderful is that? Do you remember the first time you looked into their eyes? Maybe it caused you to be a little scared (*How will I be able to take care of this little one?*) or overjoyed (*I can't believe I'm actually a mommy!*) or both—or anything in between. Nevertheless, you were called (chosen, specially equipped) to be their mom, just as Mary was called to be Jesus's mother. Everything you've gone through to this point has brought you here. You've gained strength, wisdom, and so much more to help bring them up to be who they were made to be. Through it all, there will be joys, tears, laughter, and sorrow. God has laid out a beautiful path for them, a path we cannot see and may never understand. They will go through good times and bad times, and you'll be able to help guide them through. God's plan and beautiful purpose, which He has so lovingly put together for them, will play out. But remember, Mama, it's God's plan, not yours, for their lives. He's given you an amazing task and opportunity to raise these children to know that He is good, and He's given your children an amazing task too—to fearlessly live out the plan He has for their lives. But know, Mama, that through it all, He's by your side, and He made you for this!

 *Let's face it, being a mom is full of responsibility. It's tough yet rewarding. We need God's strength more so some days than others. Through it all, know that God is working in and through all things for not only you but also for your kids (and everyone else in the world)—from the beginning of time to the end. He has so many wonderful purposes and blessings planned for your children. What a gift it is that He thought of you to be their mom! You've got this!*

Spilled Milk

"I have said these things to you, that in me you may have peace. In the world you will have tribulation. But take heart; I have overcome the world."

JOHN 16:33

As a mom of three myself, I know that some days feel more chaotic than others. It usually happens all at once . . . when you hit snooze too many times, and then the milk gets spilled, and now you're late getting the kids to school. But, Mama, you were made for this. God has put you here, with these little or big ones, to be their leader, their guide, their source of mama love and strength. You were meant to bring them up in this world as their mom. They learn from you, from how you react and what you do. We may often let our stresses and frustrations out in negative ways, but take heart. You are not alone in this. When the days get long, frustrating, and hard, take it to the Lord instead of shouting it out. Talk to your Father and allow Him to guide you to manage frustrating times and be the best mom you can be. There's no use crying over spilled milk—that can be cleaned up!—but how we act in the moment will create a lasting impression. Mistakes happen. Even chaotic times happen in public, but we must put aside our concern over what others may be thinking and be aware of our own child's feelings. Some days we need

God's strength to get through. The good news is, He's always there for us. He knows your child—and He knows you too. He's your Father, and He wants what's best for you!

 *What's frustrating you the most these days? Is there anything you wish you had said or done differently this week? In these times, remember to give yourself grace. We've all been there, and we all need Jesus! When we are weak, He is strong for us. Take whatever is on your heart and bring it to Him. Pray for guidance, wisdom, and strength. And when things get chaotic—and they will!—take a step back, breathe, and take it to the Lord.*

Pause and Breathe

"Be still, and know that I am God."

PSALM 46:10

Let's face it—we've all reached our breaking points before. We've all raised our voices, slammed doors, cried out of anger, and maybe even canceled evening plans because we hit our allotted amount of stress and frustration for the day. And while we all have different factors that set us off, we've all had those moments when enough was enough. We are, after all, human.

No one feels good about losing it. And for most of us, it takes five to ten minutes before the regret and mom guilt kick in because we know we didn't handle the situation correctly. And the truth is, Mama, your kids are watching how you react, and they are learning from you. Now, you have to give yourself grace. You can take a moment for a deep breath, calm down, apologize for your actions, and try your best to do better next time. And then when you start to feel as if you are on the brink again, try finding an empty room, pause, take deep breaths, and ask God to help you through it. Remember, Mama, spilled milk may be big in the moment, but having a lens of grace with your kids and with situations you face can help you live more like Jesus. Remember that He is in control and can change your perspective and your response. His presence can take you from a place of extreme stress and frustration to a place of serenity and strength.

It's okay, Mama. No, this wasn't your best moment. This isn't one for the scrapbooks. But in the long run, your children will remember how you made them feel over the 18 (or more) years of their childhoods. They will look back and see the few times you lost it as just that—the few times that Mom lost it. So breathe and take in God's grace, and next time, remember to pause, be still, and know that God is in control.

You are a mother, and you are human. There are going to be moments when you lose your patience and feel overwhelmed. It's just going to happen! The good news is you can tap into God's love and patience anytime, and He will lend it to you. And when He gives you grace for the moment, He enables you to pass it on to your family. These moments don't define who you are, and they don't define what kind of mother you are. Remember God is using your motherhood journey to bring you closer to Him, so you are growing and learning too. This was just a learning moment—nothing more, nothing less.

They Grow Up So Fast

"Before I formed you in the womb I knew you,
and before you were born I consecrated you;
I appointed you a prophet to the nations."

JEREMIAH 1:5

At a birthday party the other day, I saw a little boy with curly hair going down the slide. I had to do a double take because I was pretty certain that was my son, Jackson. But wait, Jackson is seven years old now, not three . . . When I made that realization, I had to hold back the tears because he looked *just like* my little guy—only when he was much younger.

Time is flying by much faster than we think. A few years back, I took my kids to Chick-fil-A, and we had a picnic on the church lawn right next door. They were very little—just two and four years old. As we ate, a woman about my mom's age came up to us and out of the blue said, "Enjoy these days. They grow up so fast. I know it can be hard now, but you're doing great." I looked at her with tears in my eyes and said, "How did you know I needed to hear that?"

Her words are true—time *is* moving fast! Enjoy all the little moments with your little ones. Put down your phone and join them in running around the yard or read them a couple of extra stories. In time, they'll want to be off playing with their friends, then off to school, then off on their own. They may not remember the book you read them or that picnic on the lawn, but they'll always remember how you made them feel. Soak up the good times in your memory bank too, Mama, because life is moving fast.

You can't go back in time, only forward. No matter if your children are still forming in the womb or are parents of their own, take the time now to realize that time moves fast. Spend as much time with them as you can—it won't be time wasted. Often, we feel so busy in the moment, but for the time we can spend, let's make it last. Let your kids be kids, as you are reminded in I Corinthians 13:11 that they will give up their childish ways someday. In the meantime, let them be little and enjoy them at every stage of their lives.

The Comparison Game

Finally, brothers, whatever is true, whatever is
honorable, whatever is just, whatever is pure,
whatever is lovely, whatever is commendable,
if there is any excellence, if there is anything worthy
of praise, think about these things.

PHILIPPIANS 4:8

Often, we can be the hardest on ourselves. We all have some degree of mom guilt, with the "she's a better mom than I am" negative self-talk. But, Mama, you are worthy. Remember the words of Philippians 4:8, and instead of letting the negative self-talk creep in, fill your mind instead with positive self-talk, replacing the negative with the good. Instead of comparing your child's birthday party to a "Pinterest-perfect party" and feeling unworthy, replace that thought with praise to God for being able to host a party that your child enjoys. Instead of comparing yourself to strangers on the internet (and their highlight reels on social media), know that they are just highlights, not real life. Behind every social media account's perfectly styled kitchen, kid's art project, and more, there's often a mess behind the camera (guilty here!). We need to stop the comparison game because it only makes us feel terrible inside. Instead, we can take those beautifully curated photos as inspiration for our own homes or parties but not as an attainable lifestyle. Our comparison even goes off social media to real life—as we look at the other moms in our kids' classes and more. We need to realize that God has placed each of us right where we need to be. We can't all be homeroom moms or even dressed perfectly each day. Just as we compare ourselves to others, our children are probably doing the same or will someday too. Stop this negativity at the source and help them (and yourself!) realize that God made each of us unique, just as we are. Let's replace the negative thoughts with grace and thankfulness.

This week, try to catch yourself when you see another person's photo, video, or social media post that makes you compare yourself or your home or situation to theirs. How does such a comparison make you feel? Can you take out the jealousy and replace it with pure thoughts? Maybe you can enjoy that image or idea without comparing it to your own situation, putting yourself in a negative light. If any negative or jealous thoughts creep in, practice replacing them with something worthy of praise, something pure, or something lovely instead—like inspiration for your next party or a new recipe to try!

Anxious Mama

Do not be anxious about anything,
but in everything by prayer and supplication
with thanksgiving let your requests
be made known to God.

PHILIPPIANS 4:6

L et's start by reading the Scripture verse above a few times, just to let it sink in. I come from a long line of women who were anxious and worried . . . how about you? Anxiety is a part of my everyday life, but this Scripture helps to remind me that God sees all my worries. We can come to Him at any time and share that anxiety with Him. But, Mama, He already knows what's on your heart. Coming to Him, as your Father, and bringing whatever has taken over your mind with worry and anxiety helps us let it out. So let your requests be known, realizing that God is already working it all out. Maybe while growing up, you recited the Lord's Prayer in church—we need to recall the words, "Thy will be done." As we raise our kids, we must remember it's God's plan, not ours. What if we lived in the posture of surrender instead of a posture of anxiety? What if we surrendered our worries, plans, and thoughts to God as we're called to do? As His will is accomplished in our lives, remember that God is trustworthy—He's the Creator of the universe, after all! He knows there will be times of worry, and He wants to make sure you know He has you and your kids safely in His hands.

Can you remember when you were a few years younger and what you worried about? Did those worries ever come true? What would you tell your younger self today, knowing what you know today? Was it worth the time spent worrying, or would you have rather just trusted God and lived a little easier at the time? God wants us to lean on Him, trusting in Him and not on our own understanding. He tells us to not worry. So, Mama, this week, let's try to do just that.

The Nudges

And the Spirit of the LORD shall rest upon him,
the Spirit of wisdom and understanding,
the Spirit of counsel and might, the Spirit
of knowledge and the fear of the LORD.

ISAIAH 11:2

As moms, we often are the ones watching out for our kids, planning their activities, and making sure each day runs smoothly. Sometimes, when we're in the middle of something—or even out of the blue—we get a nudge. You know the ones—those urges to "go over there" or "say this," and you feel a little unsettled in your soul until you finally give in and do what you knew you should have in the first place. It's important to listen to those nudges, because they could be more than just your mama instincts telling you to: *Go check on your son . . . Make sure to check the lock on the back door . . . Go tell your daughter how much you love her . . .* Mama, we're not going through life alone. Before Jesus died on the cross, He said He was going to leave us with a Helper, the Holy Spirit, who would come from the Father and reveal the truth about God (John 15:26). The Holy Spirit is there to guide us and help us along the way. God knows what our kids need even when our minds are on other things—things that we may think are more important at the time . . . I can't

22

tell you how many times my children have benefited from me acting on a nudge; and who knows how many times God has saved us from the unseen because I listened to the Helper as He gently pointed me in the right direction. We can often be busy and dismiss a nudge, but God is walking beside us in our journey in motherhood. He is for us, and He is for our kids! Sometimes He may even send an "off" feeling, or something just causes us to say no to something our kid wants to do . . . Stick to what you know is best for your children. We're here to guide them, but the best news is that God is guiding us, so we can make the tough decisions knowing they are the right ones.

Mama, be ready when God says, "Move," "Go," or "Do." Even in those nudges, sometimes it can take a while for action to happen. For me, sometimes a seed is planted within me, and I don't see what God has been growing until a few years down the road. But during the journey, you just have to keep saying yes to that next step. Mama, I know you can—you were made for this!

Having Patience

And we urge you, brothers,
admonish the idle, encourage the fainthearted,
help the weak, be patient with them all.
I THESSALONIANS 5:14

As a mom of three, I know that patience is something we all need to have with each other (even the kids too!). I'm sure you've been there, Mama. There are days when the house needs to be cleaned, and someone is calling for you, needing you, all while you're trying to do something else that feels incredibly urgent. Enter grace.

We must have grace with ourselves and with our kids, and they need to have grace with us too. We all need to realize sometimes that what we're doing will never be as important as our children in that moment. And on the flip side, they need to have patience when we are simply not available at the moment. As moms, we also need to remember that children take more time to complete a task than we do (tying shoes?!), but they too need to learn, just as we did.

Remember, Mama, your kids can't always read your mind, and this is where a lot of our frustrations can come from. We've all been there, but God so graciously calls us to be patient. The moment will pass, but how we're all left after feeling and learning from that experience will last in our hearts.

 *Do you think God is patient with you?? Before you answer that, remember that He is a loving God—just as you are a loving mom. He is patient, which means He stays cool, calm, and collected even in those stressful moments that you want to pull your hair out. Mama, practice having grace with yourself and your kids this week. In the moments that could cause you to lose your cool, go to God. Pray for direction and ask what to do next. Remember, you were made for this!*

Enjoy the Little Moments

But do not overlook this one fact, beloved,
that with the Lord one day is as a thousand years,
and a thousand years as one day.

II PETER 3:8

I was watching a video with my daughter the other day. In the video, she was just a few months old, and it is so fun to look back on what she looked like at that age. The video showed what she loved to do at that age, along with her little hands and feet. I'm so glad I took that video, as I might not have remembered how tiny her hands were or what she loved to do at that time. Recording that special little moment helped me to remember it years later.

Remember, Mama, it isn't always the big moments, the lavish vacations, the amazingly planned party that can stick with you and them forever—often it is just the small, "ordinary" moments. Cuddling together on the couch to watch a good movie or taking a walk into town . . . deciding on a whim to get ice cream after dinner or going around the table to share your favorite thing from that day. There are so many small moments each day that, while ordinary, should be cherished. A laugh at the breakfast table, a smile before saying goodbye, a bedtime story or a kiss good night . . .

a trip to the store together or just going on a walk and talking about all the things. No matter if your kids are young or older, there are still so many little moments that can be created and shared.

Think back to when you were a kid. What are some of your favorite memories? What did you do? Were you making smores in the backyard or going on a surprise picnic lunch? We can create fun and lasting memories, even in the ordinary times, for them and for us too. This week, try to stop in the little moments of the day—maybe close your eyes and listen to your kids playing games, or take a moment at the dinner table tonight and soak it all in. The days are long, but the years are short. If your kids are no longer at home, break out those photos and videos that you took—and take a trip back down memory lane.

Be
Still
and
Know

Their Story

"For I know the plans I have for you,"
declares the LORD, "plans for welfare and
not for evil, to give you a future and a hope."

JEREMIAH 29:11

How amazing is it that your children were thought of by the Lord before they were ever born? God has so many wonderful purposes for their lives. They too have a story to tell. Just like your purpose is different from another's, theirs will be too. We have to remember, Mama, that it's not about what we want for them, but it's about what *God* wants for their lives. They may like things we don't or go down paths we never intended, but God is seeing them through it all. They will have tests and trials in life, heartaches and heartbreaks, but during each of these struggles, they are being molded into the person God wants them to be. Don't worry, there will be fun and good times too, but we need our "mama strength" most when we can no longer fight their battles for them.

I was finishing the eighth grade when I lost all my best friends. The closest friends I'd had since I was young suddenly turned on me with hateful words and messages. I didn't understand why, and I was crushed, especially as we were all starting high school the next year. But now, I can look back and see God had prepared a path for me that was different from the one I was going down. He had to create a roadblock for me, to cause me to take a new way. Mama, if you find yourself or your kids in this situation, know that God is in it, even when you can't see Him at work. It may be that your child won't get into the college they hoped for or they won't make it onto a certain team, or get into a certain class, or be chosen for a certain club, but this isn't for nothing. God is preparing a much better way for them, even when you can't see it. As they grow older, you may later see how the puzzle pieces fit more perfectly together as God works out His perfect plan in their lives.

Remember, Mama, God is involved in your kids' stories. They have many purposes in life. They were made perfectly just the way they are—and they were beautifully dreamt up to love certain things and be great at certain things—it's all a part of His greater plan. We must trust in the Lord, even when we don't understand why things happen the way they do. Let's stay the course and learn to let Him lead the way, not only in our lives but in our children's too.

Letting Them Fail

Not only that, but we rejoice in our sufferings, knowing that suffering produces endurance, and endurance produces character, and character produces hope, and hope does not put us to shame, because God's love has been poured into our hearts through the Holy Spirit who has been given to us.

ROMANS 5:3–5

I f you've been a mom long enough, you've uttered the words "I told you so" or "because Mom said so" to your children. And maybe these aren't the best mom-phrases to use, but in that moment, it's all you could come up with because you told them *no* and they insisted on a reason why. Or maybe you spoke those words after your child rejected all eight of the real reasons you were giving them as to why they had to do something, but how could they possibly argue with the tried-and true "because I told you so"?

It's in these moments when we moms can sometimes come to our wits' end. We can take a good lesson from Romans 5, which tells us suffering produces endurance, and that produces character and hope. Wow, Mama, isn't this a good reminder? When we are being pushed beyond our limits, let's look past the situation at hand and to the lesson God is teaching us.

It's also good to note that our children are going to have frustrations and setbacks. In fact, what do you think would happen if your child got everything they ever wanted, never missed the mark, or never "failed" at anything? Working hard and pushing through builds character and hope. It's okay for these moments to happen. We can't do the work for them; it's up to them to push through. Sometimes we have to reach into our faith roots to remember it will work out in the end for us—and for them.

The next time your child experiences a shortcoming, no matter their age, take it in stride and with grace. The world isn't over! Help guide them to know what we're reminded of in Romans 5. Like the old saying goes, if you fall off the horse, you should get right back on! In the same way, if they didn't make the team, or if they didn't study hard enough for the exam, character can be built in these and many other moments. We often look to blame others for our child's shortcomings, but instead of yielding to this temptation, choose to build their character and give them hope for the future. Remember, Mama, you were made for this!

Identity: "Mom"

Therefore, if anyone is in Christ,
he is a new creation.
The old has passed away;
behold, the new has come.

II CORINTHIANS 5:17

We hold many titles: mom, wife, sister, coworker, (your job title), friend . . . but—spoiler alert—even though these may be the roles you possess (and you probably hear "Mom" the most!), they aren't what make you, you. It's true, God has put you where you are to have these titles, but He doesn't want you to be defined by them. Your true identity is found in and through Him—it's found in being a child of God. Yes, you have several roles on this earth—one of which is to be a mom, and what a gift that is! But that isn't where your true worth lies.

Sometimes it feels as if being a mother is our everything—it takes over our thoughts, time, and heart. So it's easy to start believing that being "Mom" defines our entire existence. Sometimes we find ourselves so deep into the mom zone that we forget we had lives before kids arrived. But the truth is we are multifaceted individuals, created uniquely by God with inherent strengths, talents, and purposes that extend far beyond what we can currently imagine.

Do you remember who you are outside of being a mom? Do you remember the younger you? What did she love to do? What brought her joy? We can't place our identity in what we do, or we'll lose ourselves and forget Whose we are. Learn to lean on Him, and know He is holding you in His mighty hands.

Think of all the titles you hold. Did you ever consider one of them to be a "daughter of the King"? He made you unique—just the way you are. Take a step back and remember all that He's made you great at. Remember the younger you—including what brought you joy. This week, step back and refocus. Put "child of God" first on your list of titles and let the rest flow from there.

Remembering Who You Are

For we are his workmanship,
created in Christ Jesus for good works,
which God prepared beforehand,
that we should walk in them.

EPHESIANS 2:10

In the last devotion, we were reminded that first and foremost, we are children of God and He created each of us perfectly unique. Then, I challenged you to remember what brought you joy as a child and encouraged you to make time for yourself. So did you do it? It's okay, you can be truthful. No judgment here.

The issue with making time for things is that most of us don't have the time to spare. We can get so busy running kids to sports practice, making work deadlines, pursuing activities upon activities, that when we finally do get to sit down, well, doing absolutely nothing for two minutes is what brings us the most joy. So, how can we make time to do what we love, to pull out our watercolors and easel or take a long bike ride or hang out with friends? The answer isn't easy. It's another "to do" on your list. But it's so important to make time *for you*. Even if it means stopping by the lake each morning on the way to work to drink your coffee, enjoy the view, and talk to God for ten minutes—those ten minutes could change the trajectory of your entire day! And while you're sitting with Him, ask Him to bring you joy throughout the day, ask Him how to add "me time" to your calendar, ask Him to take away all the mom guilt and all the worries that are clouding your mind.

Also, did you know you can find peace on your busiest day by whispering a prayer on your way into that important meeting, or thanking God for the sunshine on your face as you walk across the parking lot into the grocery store? You can lean into God's rest and tap into His joy anytime, anywhere.

Here's the deal—if you can, make time to do what brings you joy. You'll find that when you do, it will refresh your spirit and recharge your soul, and maybe even uplift the atmosphere in your home. But if you can't, God is still with you. He will never leave you. Don't forget to call on Him throughout your days.

Mama, you are an incredible woman! Be careful not to get so caught up in the daily struggles of mom life that you forget to enjoy life. Take a moment to sit back and remember what you used to love to do and what you love to do now. Embrace those passions! Nurture them! When you do, you'll be a radiant example of living a full, joyful life for your children to follow.

The Good Work

Train up a child in the way he should go;
even when he is old he will not depart from it.

PROVERBS 22:6

Mama, you need to hear this: You are putting in the good work each and every day. Often, we can see each day as the same, day after day, but they all add up—just as the years just keep coming. The days can be hard, and exhaustion can set in, but raising the next generation is a lot of *good* work. Just as our parents had to learn to navigate new challenges, we do too. And as technology advances and society changes, there is a lot to handle, Mama. But throughout all time, the Bible has remained the same. Teaching our children that there is a loving God who has a wonderful plan and purpose for them is such a great reminder, especially when things don't go as we hoped or expected.

Each family is different, but instilling love, care, and prayer into your kids and helping them to put God first, others second, and themselves third will grow them up into good humans who care about others and seek the Lord in all they do. You can start small—with prayers at bedtime or at the dinner table, thanking God for what you did that day and praying for others. Think of ways you can help your children learn more about God and Jesus, even in the small moments. Teach them to trust in His plans over their own, to follow Him all their days, and to put Him first—even when the days are long.

 *Let's face it. Raising children is a lot of good, hard work, with lots of tears, laughter, joy, and sorrow. Through it all, let's remain focused on God, on His plan for our kids' lives, and on helping them to learn to fear and love the Lord. Let's make sure they know He is always there for them and that His plans are so much greater than any we could imagine. Demonstrating your relationship with the Lord in front of your kids, and starting small, will only lead to great things in their lives.*

The World

We know that we are from God,
and the whole world lies in the power of the evil one.
1 JOHN 5:19

The book of 1 John shares a scary truth, that this world lies under the power of the enemy. Fortunately, we can look to Romans 12:2 to shed some light on this fact: "Do not be conformed to this world, but be transformed by the renewal of your mind, that by testing you may discern what is the will of God, what is good and acceptable and perfect." So, we are God's children, but the world in which we live is broken, imperfect, and something to which we should not conform. This becomes clear when we realize we are tested each day in how we respond to the world—and to our children as well. How can we live like Jesus in today's world? First things first, Jesus went to the sick, the broken, those who were pushed away from society, those needing to hear God's Word and see it in action. Our society often labels it "uncool" to follow God's Word or instruction, which can cause humans to stray or go the opposite way. We're reminded in 1 John 2:15–17: "Do not love the world or the things in the world. If anyone loves the world, the love of the Father is not in him. These are the evil things in the world: wanting things to please our sinful selves, wanting the sinful things we see, being too proud of the things we have. But none of those things comes from the Father. All of them come from the world. The world is passing away. And everything that people want in the world is passing away. But the person who does what God wants lives forever." (ICB).

 Mama, take another look at the Scripture passages in this devotion. What does their instruction look like for you and your children? How can you help them to act more like Jesus each day? Often, we have to release every earthly thing we are attached to, including our own plans for our lives, in order to make way for the plans God has for us. We have to put away our love for the things of this world such as material wealth and possessions, selfishness and greed, and ego-driven ambitions, and instead embrace God's way of humility, generosity, and contentment. His ways are best—because while worldly things may bring us instant happiness, they will all disappear, but God's love for us brings us deep joy and lasts forever!

Strong and Courageous

"Have I not commanded you?
Be strong and courageous.
Do not be frightened, and do not be dismayed,
for the LORD your God is with you wherever you go."

JOSHUA 1:9

We mamas often need strength—sometimes we need that deep God-strength to get through the day. Because being a mom isn't for the weak. Because raising children isn't for the faint of heart. It's hard work. But you really only have two choices—you can fold under the pressure, or you can ask God to lend you His strength. And the good news is He gives it to us freely. In fact, He is basically asking in Joshua 1:9 *why would you live any other way?* So, why are we living in fear of entering our teenagers' room? God says *don't be afraid. You're not alone. I'm going in there with you. We got this.*

We all want to help our children grow . . . but the truth is, God is using our roles as parents to grow us as well. He is strengthening our faith, showing us what it truly means to be selfless, asking us to trust Him more than ever, and revealing to us what it is like to love unconditionally. And as we are growing, our children are looking to us to learn how to navigate life in this world. So really, we have no choice.

Because when we remain strong and courageous in our faith, we are teaching our children Who to turn to when they need to be brave. We are teaching them they are not alone and that the God of the universe will give them the strength and courage they need to face anything that might come their way today, tomorrow, and the rest of their lives. And if we can pass this knowledge on to our kiddos, then another day of feeling like the most unfair referee who ever existed, inept at settling sibling squabbles, is worth it. Because at the end of the day, if our kids come away from this with a real relationship with Jesus Christ and strong foundation in their faith, there's nothing better or more important than that.

Mama, you are much stronger than you could ever imagine. How wonderful it is that God is right there with you in your life each day. But what's even more amazing is that He's there for everyone else too—even your kids. Let Him lay the path, plan, and foundation He has for you and your family. When you are weak, lean on Him for strength. Let your children see how you love the Lord and begin to mirror you in that way. You are strong and courageous!

Finding Community

And let us consider how to stir up one another to love and good works, not neglecting to meet together, as is the habit of some, but encouraging one another, and all the more as you see the Day drawing near.

HEBREWS 10:24–25

What does your "circle" look like? Often, after we graduate from school, it's hard to find community and make new friends. Today, social media and the internet make it a little easier to connect with other mamas around town, and for churches and nonprofit organizations to host online communities and Bible studies.

Whether your "circle" meets online or in-person, having a group of moms to talk to is helpful. When we are vulnerable and share our struggles and challenges with those in the same season as us, many times we'll find that others are dealing with similar problems. And that, my friends, is freeing, especially if you've been stuck in the mindset that you're the only one feeling a certain way.

Does it ever feel like you are alone in this mom journey? Maybe it's time to reach out to the women's group at a local church. Or maybe you feel more comfortable finding an online group. If there aren't many ways to connect in your area, why not host a get-together—even a small one? Just invite a few other moms over, plan some icebreakers, put out the snacks and drinks, and watch how it brings others together!

made for this

How do you feel about your own community? Sometimes people jump at the opportunity to connect, but other people are more reluctant to join groups or even share about themselves. When you get plugged into a community who cares and you're able to let your guard down, though, amazing things can happen. Consider using this book to start a Bible study group that brings moms together. You could read a devotion a week, share snacks or a potluck dinner, and talk about what you've learned while engaging in community. It's amazing what you can take away from others when you are open to it—you never know the wonderful things that can be in store, even years later, if you start today.

Having It All Together

Whatever you do, work heartily,
as for the Lord and not for men.

COLOSSIANS 3:23

Have you ever compared yourself to strangers on the internet or to other moms you know? Okay, I think we can all raise our hands here. It's hard not to compare, right? We think to ourselves, *Her house is so clean and spotless, and my house is chaotic and cluttered . . .* Or we think, *All the other mothers at games or drop-offs look like they must have gotten up at 5 a.m., finished a workout, showered, and dressed to the nines, while I'm here hiding behind my sunglasses, with a postpartum body, ponytail, and sweatpants.* It's easy to assume that other moms have it all together and we don't. We compare ourselves to that one snapshot we witnessed of a mom who happened to be at the top of her game that day, and we think to ourselves, *I'll never be as good of a mom as she is.*

Comparing yourself to others didn't just start when you became a mom, am I right? For many of us, it started a long time ago when we were growing up. Maybe you'd think, *See how your brother gets good grades—why don't you?* or, *Your sister finished her dinner, but you didn't.* Or maybe you felt it in school: *Those girls are getting boyfriends, so why not me?* Unfortunately, comparing ourselves to others is human nature. And when others succeed in one way or another and we don't, we're jealous. If you're struggling with this today, can I just extend a hug? It's so easy to get caught up in the comparison game, and it's a hard place to be. Try to remember that none of us is perfect, and we can't all be the same. We aren't meant to be. We all have our own strengths. Remember, the work you're doing is not for people, but for the Lord. And He isn't concerned about your messy house or your messy bun. God is looking at your heart, and He sees you. He knows how hard you're working, and He is cheering you on.

Today, extend grace—to yourself, to others, and to your children. Know that you do not have to have it all together, and they don't either. We're all trying the best we can, but some of us are more gifted at certain things than others are, and vice versa. We are all different—but each of us is fearfully and wonderfully made. We can celebrate our differences and be who God made us to be.

Be Strong and Courageous

Put Down Your Phone

"You shall not make idols for yourselves
or erect an image or pillar, and you shall not set up
a figured stone in your land to bow down to it,
for I am the LORD your God."

LEVITICUS 26:1

When you think of idols, what comes to mind? Something like the statues or pillars referred to in Leviticus 26:1? The truth is, "idols" are anything we "idolize"—whatever takes our attention away from God. Are you fixated on your love for money and possessions? Do you revere or hold people and things in higher regard than you hold God? If so, you may be falling into the trap of honoring false gods.

There are many "idols" in this world today fighting for our attention, including (but not limited to) entertainment, pleasure, fame, money, power, selfishness, and instant gratification. For example, I'm sure each of us has a phone with us literally 24/7. When we're bored, we pull out the phone. When we wake up, we pull out the phone. When we go to bed, we pull out the phone. When we're with our kids, we pull out . . . yep, the phone.

What would life look like *without* your phone? Of course, at first, it would feel uncomfortable (and maybe even cause a little panic) to go about your day-to-day life. After all, we rely on our phones to tell us what time it is, how many steps we've taken, and how to get places. But if we allow our phones to take up the majority of our time, that leaves little to no time for God. And if we are finding time to scroll social media for hours but can't find an opening in our schedule to spend a moment with God, then it's possible we are placing entertainment over our relationship with our Creator. Not to mention, mamas, your kids need to know they matter.

Take some time today to ask God if your phone (or anything) is becoming an idol in your life. Ask Him to clearly point out all that is holding you back from Him. Follow His lead and "Draw near to God and He will draw near to you" (James 4:8 NKJV).

Mama, technology will forever be changing. While we don't know what will come next, we do know that our children need to learn how and when to engage with their devices. Are you noticing that devices are taking the place of family conversations? Maybe it's time to make a change, put down the technology, talk to each other, and spend time together! And just watch what happens next! Prioritizing time for God and each other will help you live a freer, less worrisome life.

Allow Them to Be Their Age

When I was a child, I spoke like a child,
I thought like a child, I reasoned like a child.
When I became a man, I gave up childish ways.
I CORINTHIANS 13:11

Your kids will only get one childhood, and there are no redos (It is a scary thought, Mama. I'm with you here.). They are going to go through so much change and transition during the eighteen years they are under your roof. Elementary school will bring challenges such as bullying and navigating friendships; junior high brings both academic and peer pressure; and high school brings college and career planning along with dating. And on the way, they learn and become who they're made to be. Through all the stages of their lives, we have to let them be their age. And if we interfere with this process too much, or too little, it could be to their detriment.

I think it's hard for all parents when navigating the give-and-take of how much to do for our children versus when it's time to let them make mistakes and to ultimately learn along the way to become who God created them to be. Let's take a close look at how our Father directs our paths. Even if we were to stray, our Father stays with us. He never leaves us nor forsakes us. God listens to us and equips us to make the next right step. He encourages us to try new things. He allows us to fail. He loves us unconditionally. He sees where we are in life, and He meets us at that spot, never asking us to do anything we're not ready for. When it comes to parenting, why not go to the best Parent there is as an example?

Whatever we do, let's try to enjoy them at each stage. There's so much laughter and so many precious moments that we will cherish along the way. Let's equip them to enter the world as good humans and be able to do things on their own, yet knowing we're always here for them along the way. As they spread their wings, our hearts will grow each time they learn and evolve into who God created them to be. Delight in their journey, Mama. Just like God delights in yours.

Mama, don't wish for time to go by. Don't wish for that next step to come sooner than later, but instead, enjoy the ride that is motherhood with your children. Soak up the small moments and the large ones too. Through it all, let's be there for our children, just as God is there for us. You can help guide and direct, just as the Lord does, but if they make mistakes or fail, embrace them and help them to learn, just as you do in your own life. If they stray, never leave the door closed, just as your Father doesn't leave the door closed for you. It's a lifelong journey, Mama, and what a blessing it is!

Each Child Is Unique

*I praise you, for I am fearfully
and wonderfully made.
Wonderful are your works;
my soul knows it very well.*

PSALM 139:14

Before we begin today, let's pray together: *Lord, thank You so much for my children. They were fearfully and wonderfully made. Thank You for creating them to be unique, just as You planned. Thank You for giving me the wonderful honor to be their mother. Help me to raise them to live out their God-given purpose and follow You as their Lord and Savior. Amen.*

It wasn't until my middle daughter started to talk that I saw how unique and different she was from my son. My first son is shyer and reserved, a thinker, whereas my daughter is the life of the party and very social. We've yet to see how our third will turn out—he may be a fun mix of both. As each of my children grows, I see so many great ways God made them and how unique they are, how different from each other. Mama, we must celebrate and cultivate each of our children's unique gifts—and why God made them to be who they are! Let's not push them into things they aren't meant to do, but instead let's grow their character in the name of the Lord.

What's even more wonderful is seeing characteristics in your children that came from you or their dad, or maybe even a grandparent or two too! As we appreciate our children, let's not compare them to each other by considering one better than another, but instead realize how wonderful it is that they were created by the One Most High. As you navigate your child's unique qualities, stay in prayer for them. The prayer at the beginning of this devotion can be used as often as you'd like, and feel free to add to it too!

Mama, sit back and think of each of your children . . . what makes them, them? As they grow, do you see how they've changed or stayed the same? Can you pick out the unique talents or gifts God gave them or that have been worked on through school, sports, or work? Their uniqueness should be celebrated as we let them be who God created them to be. Maybe, Mama, you're already seeing that play out in the jobs they have today or the things in which they're interested. Let them follow their own path as it leads to the greater purpose in life God has for them!

Taking Time with Each Child

For everything there is a season,
and a time for every matter under heaven.

ECCLESIASTES 3:1

Having three kids myself, I know how hard it is to get one-on-one time with each child separately. When I get to have a girls' day with my daughter, it's so amazing and wonderful to spend time just with her. When the younger kids go to sleep, my oldest stays up a bit, and sometimes even wants to cuddle with his mama! While we're busy keeping up with life, housework, jobs, sports, and other activities, time spent with just one child becomes harder to find.

Even if you are a mom of one, I can imagine it's sometimes hard to put aside focused time to bond with your child in today's busy world. What if we set some time this week to plan an activity with them that they love to do—maybe that's going to the local store, taking a walk, reading a book, cuddling, or even going out to eat? When you spend one-on-one time with your child, you not only show them that they are loved and valued but also create a safe space for them to share their dreams, fears, and questions. In these moments, you have the privilege of shaping their hearts and minds, instilling values and faith, and guiding them on their journey.

It's true—time is flying by, but no matter how old your

kids are, special memories can still be made. It's not too late, so plan that date, learn that video game, conduct that science experiment, or take a bike ride. After all, no matter what motherhood season you are in, from the sleepless nights of infancy to the busy years of raising children, and eventually, the bittersweet moments when your children leave the nest, you never stop being their mom. Seasons may change, but by making one-on-one time for each individual child, no matter how old they are, can help ensure that your connection to them never will.

 *Mama, do you get one-on-one time with each of your children on a regular basis? What does that look like now as opposed to when they were younger? What do you two love to do together? This week, plan a "Mommy and ___" date. I'm sure your kiddos will love spending time with their mama—no matter how big or small they are.*

How God Sees You

Blessed be the God and Father of our Lord Jesus Christ,
who has blessed us in Christ with every spiritual
blessing in the heavenly places, even as he chose us in
him before the foundation of the world, that we should
be holy and blameless before him.

EPHESIANS 1:3-4

I wish you could see yourself how God sees you—a woman of immeasurable worth, beautifully created in His image and dearly loved beyond measure. However, many of us live with an inner critic who constantly finds fault with our looks, actions, and sometimes even our accomplishments. Did you know that our inner judgments could have stemmed from the disapproval from our parents or other significant figures in our early years? And, are you aware that by being hard on ourselves, we are showing our children how to navigate their own self-worth?

Without even knowing it, we may be contributing to our children's low self-esteem, causing them to be insecure and anxious. How? When parents compare themselves to others or have a negative self-view, children tend to model this behavior. So how we feel about ourselves is important, not just to us but to our children as well.

It's important to know that when Jesus died on the cross, He took with Him any reason for you to look down on yourself. His sacrifice cleansed you completely. He compares you to no one, and delights in your uniqueness. So next time you start to hear your inner critic, remember that you are "holy and blameless" before God. Remember that the way you perceive yourself is impacting the way your children see themselves, and ask God to fill your mind with things that are true, pure, lovely, and praiseworthy. (Philippians 4:8).

Replace anything negative you are thinking about yourself with something positive. I'll go first: I know my stomach will never look the same after having three babies, but instead of focusing on that, I choose to replace that thought with Wow! I got to carry three babies! I feel so blessed to have brought them into the world. Now it's your turn—try it!

Unconditional Love

But God shows his love for us in that
while we were still sinners, Christ died for us.

ROMANS 5:8

I bet you can remember the first time you saw your child. A big smile crossed your face, and in that moment, nothing they could ever do would take away the love that was instantly sparked in your heart and soul for them. And then . . . they started to cry, then whine, then complain, then tell you no and act up in a way that made you upset. But even when you were disappointed in their actions, that love, that spark that ignited your soul when you first saw your child, never went away. We too are sinners—we tend to cry, whine, complain, say no and act up— but because of Jesus, God does not get upset with us. We are blameless before God. When Jesus died on the cross, He took away our sins. Let's extend that same grace to our children. Of course, there will be days that we will need to discipline our children, but what would it look like if we were to always discipline out of love?

Just as God loves you and will never stop loving you, you also need to make sure they know there's nothing they can do that will make you ever stop loving them. You might not always agree with them or their choices, but a mother's love extends time and measure. Letting them know this can make your bond and relationship stronger—as they know they can always tell you anything and come to you with what's on their mind, just as you can come to your own Father.

 Mama, take a look at the kind of love, care, and acceptance you show your children. Are you showing them the same unconditional love your Father has for you? Love shouldn't come with conditions—that is, "if you do this or do that, then I will love you." The same notion goes the opposite way too. We shouldn't just love God if He gives us all the things we desire or if He does certain things for us. Let's get our mind set right so we can unconditionally love our children now and forever.

Dealing with the Past

The wise woman builds her house,
but with her own hands
the foolish one tears hers down.
PROVERBS 14:1 NIV

When we look at our past, we can see that certain things that have happened to us stick with us and cause us to act in ways that damage our minds, as well as the minds of those around us (including our children). Whether it's abuse we've experienced or ways we've been brought up, certain things need to be stopped before they are passed to the next generation. It may be time for a self-soul-check to see where we need to halt what we're carrying with us before we pass it on to others, especially our offspring. Is there an issue in your past that you need to deal with in order for it not to control your present?

Just like we are reminded in Proverbs 14, we need to build our houses up, not tear them down. When our own foundation is shaken, it needs to be fixed so we'll be able to stand strong for our own homes and families. We can break what's been passed down generationally before it's passed on further.

Don't make your past an idol in your life. Take a look at Philippians 3:13: "But one thing I do: forgetting what lies behind and straining forward to what lies ahead." We're called to forget what lies behind and strain forward to what lies ahead. We must remember this and learn to forgive, mend any wounds, and forget what's behind us, no matter how painful it is. Extend forgiveness and grace where necessary, maybe even to yourself. If there are situations where more help is needed, there is no harm or shame in seeking help to better yourself for your family and children. Mama, Jesus is always there for you, always there to lend an ear. Run toward Him and forward, rather than back into the past.

Mama, our past may try to stay with us, but when we realize it, we must put plans into place to fix whatever needs fixing and be the best we can for our children. We don't want our own anxieties, worries, and fears to continue into the next generation. Conduct a soul search this week and see what needs to be mended in your own heart and soul. Make the time to do some soul-searching and soul-healing. It will be worth it—not only for you but also for your children!

Feeling Loved

Love is patient and kind;
love does not envy or boast; it is not arrogant
or rude. It does not insist on its own way;
it is not irritable or resentful;
it does not rejoice at wrongdoing,
but rejoices with the truth. Love bears
all things, believes all things, hopes all things,
endures all things. Love never ends.

I CORINTHIANS 13:4–8

I love what happens on Mother's Day, when my kids do a writeup about me at school and I get to read it when they come home! They are asked questions like: How old is your mom? What do you like doing with your mom? And—my favorite: How do you know your mom loves you? The way they answer that question shows me how they feel the most loved.

We all experience the feeling of being loved in different ways. Not everyone feels it through cuddles and hugs! Some may feel the most cherished when they hear the words or receive a thoughtful gift. When we learn what resonates with each of our children, we can tailor our expressions of love to match their unique preferences.

As moms, our ultimate goal is for our kids to always feel truly loved. To achieve this, we must look at the Bible's definition of love found in I Corinthians 13:4–8. Does your child view your love for them as "patient and kind," or do they see it as "boastful and arrogant"? Do your children view your love as "hopeful", as the core of who you are, as an enduring, solid foundation they can always depend on? Do they see it as a lifelong guarantee? Mama, it's important that our children know too that our love for them is unfailing and never ending. It's so easy to get caught up in the expectations we place on them—good grades, best behaviors, scores at the game—that we forget that the foundation of love is what they need the most. And when they get home from that tough test or that bad day or from losing the game, that we are the safe place for them to land.

 *Mama, your children will feel love in different ways. One might want more time while the other wants little notes in his or her lunch box. It's your job to look for clues and fill their hearts! And if you need to check in on what true love looks like, always remember I Corinthians 13. Does your love for your kids come across in this manner?*

Doing Things for You

And he said,
"My presence will go with you,
and I will give you rest."

EXODUS 33:14

Do you ever feel guilty about doing things for yourself? Some days I even feel guilty for having my husband be with the kids while I take a shower, or I even ask if it's okay if I do something for myself. As moms, we can get used to being the default parent, and so we put ourselves last. But the truth is, we have to take care of ourselves and our own well-being so we can take care of others—whether that's our family members or work colleagues and more. When we're drained or we need to "refuel," we can't serve others as well as we'd be able to if we were "full." In the Bible, it talks about our need for rest. We may feel guilty for actually taking time to rest—especially when the kitchen is dirty, the weeds need pulled, and there's no more milk in the fridge. We put a lot of pressure on ourselves to live up to perfection, but we need to realize things will never be perfect. Perfection is simply just not attainable, and it's okay to ask for help. We don't need to feel we have to do it all, all the time. If we carry the burden of pushing ourselves down as we keep everything else held up, it will wear on us. Take time to rest—in whatever way works for you: going for a walk, taking a shower, attending a fitness class, having dinner with an old friend, or savoring your morning coffee. When you take the time to rest, you will then be able to be the best mama you can be!

made for this

Mama, I urge you to find time to rest. When you look at yourself and your fuel tank, where does it stand? Are you running on "E" and needing to fill back up soon? Or is your tank already full? How do you refuel? What does "rest" or "recharging" look like to you? What fills your tank back up so that you have the energy and mindset to take on the day?

God goes
Beside Behind
Before you

Feeling Seen

Set your minds on things that are above,
not on things that are on earth.

COLOSSIANS 3:2

In some capacity, we all want to feel seen, understood, and liked. We spend our lives people-pleasing, wondering and worrying what others think of us—whether it's our spouse, parents, friends, strangers on the internet, or even fellow drivers on the road. Spoiler alert: We can't control other people's feelings. Not everyone will like you, just as you'll not understand or like every person you meet. We're all human. We need to give ourselves grace and be okay with who we are, knowing we can't spend our lives trying to please others. We're reminded in Colossians 3:2 that we need not worry about pleasing those on earth and instead keep our minds on things above. That ache in your heart for worth can only be satisfied in Jesus. Know that you are worthy and wonderful just as you are. Your life is found in Him, not in the acceptance of others. Your worth is found in Him, not in what others think of you. Today is a great day to release that need for validation from others. Release the need to prove yourself to others. You are already worthy and loved!

 Mama, today start to become aware of when you feel the need to be liked or validated by others. Do you seek this much validation from above? As humans, we're social creatures, and we want to treat our neighbors as ourselves, but we can't lose ourselves in the process. Instead of focusing on earthly validation, let's instead set our minds on things that are above. Release the trap you're in and be set free. Practice loving yourself for who God created you to be.

Fear and Faith

For God gave us a spirit not of fear
but of power and love and self-control.

II TIMOTHY 1:7

Raise your hand if you experience fear. If we were all together in a room, you'd see every hand up. We've *all* experienced fear. Now that we are mamas, that fear is multiplied by how many kids we have. We worry about them, about whether they're safe, okay, and doing the right thing . . . especially when Mama isn't around. But as we fear for their futures—will they pick the right careers? will they choose the right friends? will they do well in school? will they make the right choices?—it's up to us to help mold and shape them now to trust in the Lord as their guiding light.

While they're young, we are on more of a high alert to make sure they are okay—we baby-proof the house, make them wear bike helmets, and say, "Careful!" way too many times. It's not a bad thing to have concerns, as it keeps us safe as humans, and it has for thousands of years. We even get nudges from above to go check on things or tell our kids things, and those are very important to listen to and act upon. But II Timothy reminds us to replace that fear we have with self-control and with love. We can replace our fear with faith.

Now, that doesn't mean not to take appropriate measures to be safe, but more than that, we must know that God is for us. When we experience fear and things seem out of control, we need to place our trust in Him. We need to replace fear with faith and give it to God and trust Him to work things out.

Mama, if you're like me, fear can be a normal day-to-day occurrence. While some concern is appropriate at times, when we let our fear turn into anxiety, when circumstances spin out of our control, or when we become overly worried about the future, it's time to regroup. Place whatever you're fearful about into God's hands and leave it there. He holds the universe together, and He holds you together too. Take some deep breaths and know that His plans are better than our own. Trust that He will guide both you and your children—because He loves you more than you could ever know.

God First, Others Second, Me Third

And Jesus answered him,
"It is written, 'You shall worship the Lord your God,
and him only shall you serve.'"

LUKE 4:8

Have your kids ever gone to summer camp? The church where my children attend preschool hosts a great summer camp. At the end of the week, they gather all the kids in a room with the parents in the back to see what their children learned. One of the things my kids recited was this: "God first, others second, me third." *Wow!* I'm so glad they started learning this while that young (preschool to elementary age)! We need to know it ourselves and teach our children this amazing truth: We must put God first above all else. Next, others should come second. We're called to love our neighbors as ourselves, and the life and servitude of Jesus is a real testimony of how we should focus and our lives. We then come in last.

Now, don't let this shift your thinking about still needing to rest, as we learned a few devotions back, but we should continue to focus on how to be a good human. This can be done even in small ways toward others, like teaching our kids to hold doors open for others, help a neighbor in need, and even use their gifts to serve others. Finding out what gifts your children have and seeing how uniquely they've been created can help them see how they can serve others using their gifts for good.

 Mama, I hope you found the first, second, and third sayings impactful, and I hope they help you teach your children to focus on God and put others before themselves. Let's pray for some guidance: Lord, I come to You knowing I haven't always put You first. Help me shape my days and thoughts around You, to serve You and You alone, and not the world. Help me teach my children to focus on You and learn to serve others, just as Jesus did. In Jesus's name I pray, amen.

In the Storms

Count it all joy, my brothers, when you meet trials of various kinds, for you know that the testing of your faith produces steadfastness. And let steadfastness have its full effect, that you may be perfect and complete, lacking in nothing.

JAMES 1:2–4

Have you ever sat on the beach and watched the waves come in and out? Day in and day out, the waves come, sometimes gentle and caressing the shore, other times powerful and roaring. Just like these waves, life has its own rhythms and cycles, with moments of calm and turbulence. But no matter how the waves change, the ocean remains constant—powerful, vast, boundless, deep, serene, tranquil, and beautiful. And just like the ocean, God remains right there with us during the calm seasons and during the raging ones. He is the steady, unchanging force who provides us with strength and guidance to navigate the challenges we face.

We're reminded in James 1 that trials will test our faith. Are you facing a trial today? Try to remember that beyond this challenge is a stronger, more resilient you. God is using this time to strengthen your faith and build endurance. There is a purpose to this pain. God has a plan for you beyond this, so look past what is right in front of you toward the powerful, vast, boundless, deep, serene, tranquil, and beautiful life that awaits. Remember, God will never leave nor forsake you! He's got amazing plans for your life—more than you could ever dream or imagine. So hold on tight and focus on the amazingness that is coming.

Mama, even reading this devotional will help your faith roots to grow deeper and stronger. In each trial you face, look for the positive to come out of it as you focus your gaze on Him and not what is going on around you. Put your full faith and trust in God, and He will equip you and see you through any storm. As your faith builds, others will see this in your life, and that will give you the opportunity to share your faith with them as well.

This Day

Yet you do not know what tomorrow will bring.
What is your life? For you are a mist that appears
for a little time and then vanishes.

JAMES 4:14

Mama, you won't get this day back (sad but true). Your children will never be as young as they are today. When you look back at pictures, I'm sure you can think, *Wow, that seems like just yesterday*, or, *Wow, time really flew by!* Each day can seem the same, but as we look back just a few months or years, we can see time is slipping away. James 4:14 serves as a gentle reminder that life is indeed a fleeting mist, and it encourages us to make the most of the gift of today.

As mothers, we can be consumed by worry, or by the stress of never being able to catch up at work, or by that never-ending-to-do list. We can easily become so focused on these worries and stressors that we forget the preciousness of the present moment. Let this devotion be your reminder to savor today—whether it's your daughter mastering her first cartwheel or your son joyfully dancing over a bite of ice cream. Savor each moment, and look forward to making new ones. You've been given this day—each day is a new gift, a new blessing—so make the most of it.

Another way to lose sight of the present is by wishing the

days away. Have you ever thought, *I can't wait until they're out of diapers . . . sleeping through the night . . . in school all day . . . have their own car . . . get a job . . .* and so on? Instead of wishing for time to march on, maybe ask God to help you focus on the things you love about this current season. Ask Him to help you forget about today's worries or tomorrow's possibilities, but instead on the sweet moments that are happening right before your eyes.

Years from now, you will likely wish you were back where you are today, it's true, but why is that so hard to hear at times? Is it because on the hard days when both toddlers are sick and the dishes are piled up to the ceiling and you were up all night, and someone says "Cherish these days, you'll miss them," you start to wonder as to whether that person truly understands what the last eight hours of your life entailed. Plus the immediate challenges you are facing are currently overshadowing the potential nostalgia for the present. Trust me, I get it. It's not easy. And the truth is there might be nothing about today that you will miss. Let me just say, you're doing a great job. Hang in there! Tomorrow will be better. . .

It Takes a Village

Do not forsake your mother's teaching.
They are a garland to grace your head
and a chain to adorn your neck.

PROVERBS 1:8-9 NIV

Mama, you're putting in the good work. Parenting children is not easy, and it does take a village. Between moms and dads, significant others, grandparents, aunts, uncles, and teachers . . . many people play a part in a child's life to raise them well. As they get older, more influence starts to rush in—from other children, TV shows, or what they see online. There is no shame in setting boundaries when raising your children to be who God created them to be. It's okay to say no to them watching a certain YouTube channel or not allowing them to have a phone until they're much older. We live in a broken world, and as a mom, you get so much credit for trying to do your best each day. Proverbs 1 reminds us that the teachings we share with our children will be with them throughout life. There is no shame in raising them well, to love the Lord and be a good human being. Choosing wisely who the village is that comes into their world is certainly okay, but as a mom, never forget the influence that you—and only you—have in their lives!

What is something you still need to teach your children? What did you learn from your own parents that you need to pass along or wish you yourself had learned earlier? Today, let's end this time in a prayer: Lord, thank You so much for my children. They were beautifully and wonderfully made in Your image. Help me to teach my children and bring them up as You would have me to do, Lord. Help me to keep their eyes focused on You and Your purposes for their lives. Lord, give me strength and courage each day, amen.

God's Children

For this child I prayed, and the LORD has granted me
my petition that I made to him.
Therefore I have lent him to the LORD.
As long as he lives, he is lent to the LORD.

I SAMUEL 1:27–28

Hannah, a woman of faith from the Old Testament, was barren, but she pleaded with God to have a child. The Lord answered her prayers, and her son Samuel was born. No matter how you became a mother, there were likely times when you weren't sure if your dream of motherhood would come true. Do you remember the feeling of wondering if you were going to be blessed with a child? Not knowing if you would be gifted with what your heart so deeply longed for? As mothers, it's important to remember that our children are gifts from God. Why not pause for a minute or two right now and allow your heart to fill up with love for your kiddos, and share that moment with their Creator?

Now that your heart is filled with gratitude, let's get back to Hannah. Once Hannah had Samuel, she dedicated him to God, meaning after he was weaned, Hannah took her child to the Tabernacle to live forever. What an act of surrender! She gave Samuel, the child she waited on for so many years, over to her Lord and in an act of complete trust walked away knowing that her baby was in the best hands that ever existed.

Hannah's story is an inspiring reminder of what we are called to do as moms. Embrace each day with a grateful heart, trust God to protect, love, and guide our children, and look to Him for wisdom and strength. Next time you start to question the decisions you've made as a mother, or feel as if you lost your compass, come back to the example of Hannah. Have you praised God for your kids lately? Are you trusting Him with their lives? And, are you relying solely on His everlasting love for guidance and wisdom? If the answers to these questions are a resounding *yes*, then rest assured, you are probably on the right track.

Mama, you were made to be these children's love, support, and guidance. It may have been a long journey for you to be a mom; or it might have been a piece of cake. But no matter what, you are here . . . a mom . . . and that holds such a great responsibility! Rest in the peace that God knew your child before they were ever born, and He handpicked you to be their mother. You are known and loved. You are a gift to your children and those around you. You've got this, Mama!

Waiting

*But they who wait for the L*ORD *shall renew their*
strength; they shall mount up with wings like eagles;
they shall run and not be weary;
they shall walk and not faint.

ISAIAH 40:31

I was in line with my kids the other day, and each time they asked when it would be our turn, I told them we just had to wait. Waiting is hard, even for grown-ups. Because we live in a world of instant messaging, fast food, and answers to questions right at our fingertips, we've grown used to not having to wait. But when it comes to our lives, no matter how hard we might try to make changes happen on our own, the truth is it's all in God's timing. And we're waiting for what He has in store for us, not what we have in store for ourselves.

As a younger woman, I remember waiting for my husband to arrive and then to be a mom. It felt like forever, but God's plans were much better than my own. If it had all happened as soon as I would have liked, it might have gone completely differently. God knows our hearts and what's best for us. He sends roadblocks so that we take a new and better course. He holds the universe together, and He loves you, Mama, more than you'll ever know.

So in this day and age, how do we teach our children that

waiting isn't a bad thing but that it's part of God's amazing journey for us? One way is by modeling patience—why not talk to your children about a specific situation you are waiting on today? Talk to them about how you are trusting God's plan over your own. Let them know what you are grateful for as you wait, and be sure to celebrate with them when God works it all out. We may never know or understand why the waiting happens, but we do know that God is always working. So dig deep and focus on Him rather than on the wait.

Think back to a time when you were wishing to be right where you are now . . . What would you tell yourself back then? How can you use that knowledge and strength now as you wait for what's ahead? Learn to soak up the present instead of always wanting and wishing for what's next, and seek what He wants for you instead of what you want for yourself. That can be a challenge, but when we seek His will above ours, there is no disappointment—only glory to Him as He builds our trust during the wait. He's working inside you during the waiting times, so don't waste them. What is He trying to work out through you today?

Doing Good

And let us not grow weary of doing good,
for in due season we will reap, if we do not give up.
GALATIANS 6:9

There are numerous ways to do good . . . and raising our children to know all of them will make the world a better place today and tomorrow. By modeling and sharing what it means to "do good" to our children, we are setting them up to teach the same behavior to their children and eventually, it will be passed on to their children's children.

For example, I told my son that we'd go ride bikes after dinner. However, shortly after I made this statement, he blatantly disobeyed me. While the thought crossed my mind to cancel the bike ride, I decided to show him grace instead. It is my hope that by extending grace and forgiveness to my son, he now knows how to extend it to others.

"Doing good" also means being nice to someone who isn't nice to you. While it's hard to *always* be the bigger person, it's important to respond in a manner that is pleasing to God and stay true to His good standards and practices. Even simple things like thanking a waitress for the food, letting another driver have the good parking spot, or holding the door open for a fellow mom who is struggling with her stroller can shine God's light to more than just that person; it can inspire that waitress, driver, and mom to do good to those who cross their paths.

Mama, I have a fun challenge for you and your children this week. Find some ways to "do good" to others, both at home and out in the world. Challenge your kid to talk to the boy or girl by themselves at recess . . . help out a neighbor in need . . . or give part of their allowance or paycheck to a good cause . . . How can you raise them up to be good humans? How can you help them be nice when someone isn't so nice to them? How can you all show God's love to others?

you are
loved

It's Okay Not to Be Okay

But rejoice insofar as you share Christ's sufferings,
that you may also rejoice and be glad
when his glory is revealed.

I PETER 4:13

Are you aware that it really is okay not to be okay? We've all been there—whether for an hour, a day, a week, a month, or a season. Our lives are filled with peaks and valleys. But no matter where we are, we can rest in the peace of knowing that Jesus understands what we are going through. When Jesus walked the earth, He experienced the highs and lows of life. He enjoyed spending time with His friends, He performed miraculous acts of kindness, and He seemed to have a genuine connection with nature and the outdoors. But He also experienced suffering. He was ridiculed and made fun of, had heartache, and even cried. Jesus knows, just as we do, that this is not a perfect world.

There have been many times, mostly at night, when I am not okay, but in the morning, a new day dawns, and a new page turns. It's true that God turns despair to hope and sorrow to joy. But sometimes it takes longer than we want. If you're still waiting for the dawn of a new day, don't worry. . . it will come. Try taking things one day at a time or even a moment at a time if necessary. And if appropriate, it's not always a bad idea to share your struggles with your children, just be sure to show them Who you are holding onto in the storm. What a huge testimony of faith this will be!

Each day will bring new challenges. But when we learn to surrender our plans to God's great purpose, we can accept the waves as they come, standing strong, focusing our gaze, and putting our faith in Him alone. People can and will fail us—we are all only human. Situations will not always go as planned. We must accept the hand we've been dealt and learn from each situation we experience. Remember what we learned a few devotions ago—to count it all joy when trials come our way. You got this, Mama!

It Can Wait

"So whatever you wish that others
would do to you, do also to them,
for this is the Law and the Prophets"

MATTHEW 7:12

Picture yourself in the past. You are still a little kid, and you need to tell your mom something. You have just one thing on your mind, and you need to tell her—*now*. But when you find her, she's too busy, and so you walk away . . . How do you feel? Or maybe you just wanted to play . . . but your mom was running around doing housework. How did that make "little you" feel? It's interesting to think of that perspective when your kids need you. Think of yourself as a little older . . . Maybe you have just come home from college and you want to feel "at home" after being away so long, but your parents have decided to go away that weekend instead . . . How would you feel?

Our children need us, and they always will. I still call my mom for things I need or when I have questions. My kids come up to me a lot when I'm working, and it used to really stress me out, as I like to be focused. But as I dug deeper and thought about how I might have felt as a child if my mom was too busy for me, things changed. I recognized their feelings. Whatever you're doing may be important, but is it more important than your child?

Please don't take this the wrong way—I'm not trying to pile on the mom guilt. I know there are times when we have responsibilities that require our full attention, and I know how hard it is to strike a balance with everything we juggle as moms. All I'm saying is maybe next time your child needs your attention and you're busy, ask yourself if what you are working on can wait. And if it can, it's a beautiful opportunity to show them that they are a priority in your life. Needs change over the years, but if they know that Mom is in their corner and cares to spend time with them today, you are nurturing a bond that will last a lifetime!

Mama, I have been there too . . . lots of times. I am always so busy with work and home, but this change in perspective was so helpful to me! It may not work every time, but consider how turning your gaze from what you're doing and actively listening to your child changes how you both feel. When a child feels loved and cared for by their mother, it gives them a solid foundation for a child to build confidence and self-esteem. This week, make the effort to listen to what your kids need, and tell whatever else it is that it can wait.

I'll Be Happy When . . .

You make known to me the path of life;
in your presence there is fullness of joy;
at your right hand are pleasures forevermore.

PSALM 16:11

D o you ever doubt that you're making a difference? Do you wonder if your role as a mother is really all that important? If all the late-night homework assignments, early morning sports practices, and the countless meals you've prepared are actually helping anyone? Let me assure you, Mama, that you play a vital role in the lives of your kids. In fact, you have the unique opportunity to mirror God's love and guidance to your children. You are His vessel. And just as God illuminates your own journey, you have the privilege of playing a part in God's plan to help light the way for your children.

Even when teenagers push back or express their independence, they are soaking up your values, your love, and your wisdom. Your consistent care and support provide them with a sturdy foundation to navigate the challenges of growing up—and it will determine how they face challenges as adults, and one day as parents themselves.

You see, Mama, your children are looking to you for how life should be lived. What are they seeing? Are they seeing a woman who is filled with joy and laughter even while she cleans the house? Are they experiencing your tender touch when they accidentally hurt themselves? Does your presence create an atmosphere of delight? Your job is so much more than laundry and dishes. If you look at the bigger picture, you'll find that your actions today, no matter how mundane or difficult, are guiding them, demonstrating how to confront their present and future challenges, and instilling a lifelong sense of joy. But don't worry, Mama, God is with you every step of the way. You and He are in this together!

Mama, next time you start to question whether your role is significant or wonder if you are just a side character in the grand story of life, remember this: your presence, your way of life, and your daily actions all play a huge part in God's beautifully intricate plan for your precious kiddos. You are not a mere extra in their lives; you are a leading character, a guiding force, and a profound source of love and wisdom.

Known and Cherished

Let all that you do be done in love.

I CORINTHIANS 16:14

When your children are young, they look up to you in so many ways—both literally and figuratively. They seek your approval and want to be known and cherished by you. They want you to care for them, validate their feelings, give them guidance, and comfort them in times of need. They long for you to share in their joys and their sorrows. And when they mess up, they want you to be slow to anger and eager to listen. Does this sound familiar? Think about it—isn't that exactly what our heavenly Father gives us?

Isn't it wonderful to know that when we talk to God, He gives us His full attention and listens to every single one of our concerns? When we mess up, God gives us forgiveness. He never says, "I don't know what you should do next." He either says, "Go this way," or "Wait here . . . I'll tell you when the time is right to make a move." When we take our pain to God, He meets us there and holds our hands through it, comforting our broken hearts until it's time to walk out of the darkness into the light. When we take our weaknesses to God, He reminds us to be strong and courageous because He, our almighty Father, is by our side. God knows us, and treasures us, and we know it because He listens to us, He releases us from shame, He guides us, He comforts us, and He gives us the strength and confidence we need to face each day.

As parents, we are pulled in so many different directions, but how does it make you feel that our young ones want the same love and affection from us that we get from our heavenly Father? It's a big order to fill, I know. But let's be mindful of this fact and respond to them as Jesus would—being there with them and for them, truly and genuinely listening, caring, playing, spending time, and enjoying them. How you treat them today is how they'll begin to treat others, and it helps build their character. Show them that they are genuinely known, seen, cared for, and loved—just as your heavenly Father has showed you so many times!

Mama, this may be something to really think through—even with your partner. No one is perfect, and I too need this reminder from time to time. Often, we can treat others outside of our households much better than our own children. Phones and other things can take our attention away from them, and they know when they aren't being listened to. Let's raise them up to know they are worthy and loved, and more important than a screen or whatever is going on in the moment.

Praying for Your Kids

*"And whatever you ask in prayer,
you will receive, if you have faith."*

MATTHEW 21:22

Did you grow up saying your prayers before bed each night? Or maybe you pray while getting ready for the day, while you're in the shower, or while driving to work. Maybe praying is new to you, or you don't know where to start (and that's totally okay too!). Praying is a quiet time between you and God, a time when you can pour your heart out and tell Him what's on your mind. You can even envision Him there with you as you fold your hands, close your eyes, and bow your head. Visualize placing what you have on your heart at His feet to take on Himself, and know it'll be taken care of.

Before your children are born and even as old as they get, praying for them is a great way to bring before God what's on your heart for every and any season of their lives. From praying for a good delivery to their choices in friends, to letting them know that God is for them, to helping heal a broken arm, to choosing the right significant other in their life . . . the options are endless and so unique to each person and family. Including your kids in your prayers, and even praying for them outside of your specific daily prayer time, is such a wonderful habit. You can take it a step further and teach your child to pray as well. Praying together as a family is a great way to help your kids learn how to talk to God and show them that it can be anytime—not just at night or before eating, etc.

God is always there for them, no matter the time of day! Just the same, He's always there for you too, Mama, so come to Him without reservation. He already knows your heart, even deeper than you do, so let it all out!

Mama, take a moment to consider what's on your heart when it comes to your children. What do you want to bring before the Lord, not only to help them but also to help you as their mama? What does your prayer life look like? How can you pray for your children's needs now and in the future? Praying for their future friends, significant others, and even spouse is great, no matter how small your children are right now. Let them see you praying and get them involved! Do you have a nightly prayer routine you can start with your children or even at the dinner table? This week, Mama, let's pray!

Celebrate with Them

So now faith, hope, and love abide, these three;
but the greatest of these is love.
1 CORINTHIANS 13:13

Love is the cornerstone that enables us to share in our children's happiness. On a daily basis, I hear, "Mommy! Mommy! Look at this!" as my daughter shows me a creation she's proud of, or a new discovery she's made. I love her using her God-given gifts and how much joy it brings her—my heart can't help but be immersed in her enthusiasm. As a mom, I cherish the times that I get to experience childlike joy with her. When I am celebrating in my children's happiness with them, the weight of the world rolls off my shoulders and all my stress fades away. Their joy lifts me up! It's as if God whispers to my heart, "Here is a piece of My joy, wrapped in the laughter of your child. Take a moment to unwrap it, cherish it."

God creates moments for us to delight in our children every single day, whether it be in their artwork, their stories, the home run they made at the baseball game, or the A they made on the test, these are all gifts from the Creator—gifts that should be celebrated! In fact, God delights in us as His children. "He will rejoice over you with gladness . . . he will exult over you with loud singing" (Zephaniah 3:17). When we celebrate their wins, it lets our children know that we care about them, and that we are on their side. Let's not let these opportunities pass us by! Share the joy your children have today—it's one of the best ways to show them how much you truly love them.

Mama, your children bring such joy to you! Today is a great reminder to help celebrate in their joy—no matter how big or small—their happiness and their wins. And if it so happens that your children don't feel as if they have anything to celebrate today, help them find that joy! Ask them questions about what they enjoyed about their day, about their favorite friends, and about what they are looking forward to tomorrow? And don't forget to celebrate their answers with them.

Work Hard

Whatever you do, work heartily,
as for the Lord and not for men.

COLOSSIANS 3:23

Let's face it, Mama: Mom work is hard work! And when we add on all the other responsibilities of life to our mom duties, we can feel weighed down. It's important to remember that we're not working for just our families, but we are working for the Lord. Colossians tells us that every task we have, and in everything we do, we are to do it "heartily" and to do it "for the Lord." So it doesn't matter if you are running a financial report at work, cleaning up the kitchen after dinner, or running on the treadmill—every single thing you do is considered God's work.

We all have those tasks we don't like to do. It's hard to work "for the Lord" when we find the job to be boring or needless. However, if you take people and places out of the equation and remember that you are completing this task for God, that can change your entire outlook on the situation. All of a sudden you realize that there is a bigger purpose behind your efforts— a purpose that may not be clear at the moment, but you know that if the work you are doing is for God then He is using it in His big plan to work all things out for your good and the good of others.

Maybe you're like me too, and after a day of work and kids and constantly cleaning up, there's no applause or hearts full of thankfulness . . . yet we do it all again tomorrow. So, Mama, take heart and know that you're doing a great job, even if you feel like there are days when you're not up to par. Perfection is never attainable. Work hard and put your heart into all the tasks. Jesus is the One who sees and knows and appreciates everything you do!

Mama, you aren't alone. God sees what you do every day! Let this also be a reminder to recognize others' hard work and give them an "atta girl" or an "atta boy" every now and then. Find ways this week to also thank those who help you in this motherhood journey for all they do. Let's encourage each other and say, "God sees you, and I see you too. Thank you for working hard!" You can instill this in your children too by thanking them for making their bed or doing their homework, even teaching them to thank others as well. Let's create a thankful generation that knows the value of working hard and that we're ultimately working for the Lord.

People In, People Out

For everything there is a season,
and a time for every matter under heaven.

ECCLESIASTES 3:1

I don't know about you, but I hate yard work. I leave that up to my husband, since he's much better at it. But something he taught me is that if you prune the rosebushes and pick off all their dead leaves and branches, they'll keep producing flowers all season long. Did you ever realize that God does this in our lives? He's the ultimate Gardener. He will prune people in and out of our lives. He makes the pathways straight for us.

I remember just before high school started, many of my friends were pruned away by God. I didn't understand why—these had been my best friends growing up—but then I got mean emails from them making fun of me right before we started high school. I didn't know where to turn except to God. During those days I became closer to Him than I ever had before. So this awful experience ended up greatly impacting my life in a positive way.

Because I was bullied, I knew what it was like to feel alone in this world. So as an adult, when I started my own business (Sweet Water Decor) it wasn't long before I decided that each message we placed on our products would be motivational and inspirational. Today, Sweet Water Decor has sent hundreds of thousands of products and gifts with uplifting and affirming messages into the world. It started as a calling from God years before it ever happened, and it turned into an amazing small business where we bring light into others' lives through our products and candles. God had a plan.

Sometimes not-so-nice people enter our lives. We may wonder, *Why, God, why would You have me go through this?* But in time, we can see that God creates beauty out of ashes. He sees the whole picture, when we just see the current circumstances. We must learn to build ourselves and our kids up, to not put our worth in what others say to us or what they think of us. Take it all in stride, for God's plan is always best!

Mama, God brings people in and people out—for our good. We can see this with our children: They'll go through different friends or boyfriends/ girlfriends, and new people will come into their lives. You may see something similar happen with bullies or not-so-nice people, and it's all too common, even in our lives as adults. Build up yourself and your children to withstand the storms of others and redirect your value and worth as from God rather than from imperfect humans.

The Right Path

Train up a child in the way he should go;
even when he is old he will not depart from it.

PROVERBS 22:6

Proverbs 22 says to equip our children with an unwavering faith. And isn't that the goal? Because if they love God and they have a personal relationship with their Savior, then we know, as parents, that they have something solid on which to stand. And in the end, their faith is the only thing that will stay with them—and be passed on to their children, and their children for generations to come. Having a strong faith doesn't mean that life will be easy for our children. But it does mean that they will always turn to God and He will be there for them, walk with them, and set them on the right path.

We want our children to know that God is for them, that He'll never leave them, and that even through the good times and the bad, there is a purpose for everything. We want them to know this because we've witnessed His goodness in our lives, and we want the same for our kids. We want them to know that they can rely on God during harsh circumstances, and they can give their stresses to God during overwhelming days. We want them to know they don't have to worry, because He has got it all handled, even when roadblocks and setbacks come.

There are so many lessons to teach our kids—how to be kind, be a good sport, eat with your mouth closed, make a bed, establish good study habits—but none of these are going to get them through the ups and downs of life. Let's be sure to be parents who train our children to put God first. While the choice to believe is ultimately in their hands, we can do our part as moms to share our testimonies, to point out His faithfulness in our day-to-day lives, and to surround them with people and places that will encourage them to trust in God. And Proverbs says if we do this, they will not depart from their faith, even when they are old.

Mama, it is hard raising children! Each one is different, and the ways of the world can take over, no matter the age and time in life. Today, let's end our devotional in a prayer: Lord, thank You so much for my children. Thank You for creating them and having a wonderful purpose for their lives. Lord, help me to guide them each day to lean on You and not on their own understanding. Help me to train them up in the way they should go, to glorify You, Lord. You know their hearts, so please be with them through every step of their lives. I pray this in Jesus's name, amen.

God is working In and Through all Things

Mistakes Are Okay

Though he fall, he shall not be cast headlong,
for the LORD upholds his hand.

PSALM 37:24

Sometimes learning happens the hard way, especially when it comes to God's love for us. Unconditional love is such a hard concept for our minds to wrap themselves around. We often think that if we mess up, God doesn't love us anymore—or maybe even that God is going to get revenge on us for making the mistake. And when things don't go our way and prayers aren't answered the way we wanted, we get angry with God. But through all of our doubts and emotions, God is still there. He is gentle with us. And when we mess up, instead of waiting for God to get back at us, we can ask ourselves, *What does God want me to learn here?*

Have you ever wondered if your children are awaiting punishment from you? Or that you don't love them anymore because they made a mistake? Maybe it's time to talk to them about what unconditional love truly means. And as you share God's tenderness with them, they will learn not to be so hard on themselves but to learn from their mistakes. The old saying about falling off a horse and getting back on again is true! Sometimes kids want to quit when they make a mistake or fail at something, but it doesn't mean their life is a failure or they will never succeed. It doesn't mean that God is upset with them, and it certainly doesn't mean that you no longer love them. Teaching your children that mistakes are nothing more than good learning experiences will go a long way toward helping their confidence level and self-esteem. And teaching them that God's love and your love will never waver goes a long way toward helping them live life with a solid and true foundation.

Mama, watching your children make mistakes is not an easy thing. We try our best to guide them to make the right choices, no matter how small or big. Just as we had to learn the hard way sometimes, they may have to as well. There will be challenges, but remind them that mistakes are okay and they can learn from them. Even you and I still learn from our mistakes! We are all still learning each and every day.

Envy

A tranquil heart gives life to the flesh,
but envy makes the bones rot.
PROVERBS 14:30

I don't know about you, but scrolling through social media can bring on a case of envy, am I right? We see the mom with the perfect outfit, kids, and house. It seems like her place is always clean, and she's always so put together. Even her kids don't have a speck of dirt on them and are always dressed so well. The parties she throws look like they came straight out of Pinterest ... When we start to compare our lives to others', envy can set in. It tears us down on the inside, especially if we think we're not as good as they are or don't have what they have going on. When you start to feel this way, shut off the phone or look the other way. Take it in stride. Social media isn't real life; it's typically filtered photos and edited videos. Turn away from the envy and instead focus on what God has given *you*. Gratitude is the antidote to envy.

If you struggle with being envious of others, it might be time to consider whom you're following on social media. Why are you following them? When you look at their posts, does it bring you joy? Or does it bring you feelings of hatred? Or envy? Does this person you are following fill your bucket? Or deflate your balloon? If their page is only causing you to feel negatively toward them and in return negatively toward your life, then you may want to consider unfollowing them.

It's true that we're called not to envy, but we are all human, and we need to give ourselves grace. If you find yourself filling up with envy, don't put more on yourself by feeling guilty about being envious, instead refocus your thoughts on the many blessings you have been given, and fill your heart with gratitude and thankfulness. Many times, we envy earthly things, but these things will all fade away. Remember the wonderful things God has given you and the eternal love He has for you, and let the gratitude fill your heart, pushing out any envy or jealousy that might still be there.

Mama, it's time to take a heart check . . . how do you stand with envy? When I start to feel the jealous monster rise up, especially when I'm scrolling through social media, I turn that feeling around and look for what can I take from the photo or use as inspiration for my own life. I might not be able to dress like my friend does or have a perfectly curated home like my work colleague, but I can use it to take inspiration from over envy. And I can look around and be thankful for the blessings God has placed in my own life as well!

See Mommy Do

Rejoice always, pray without ceasing,
give thanks in all circumstances;
for this is the will of God in Christ Jesus for you.
I THESSALONIANS 5:16–18

Is there a person in your life whom you've learned from and now you see yourself mirroring with your own habits and values? Maybe it's someone in your family, maybe even your mom or grandma. Our kids also watch *us*—how we act, how we react, what we do, what matters to us, how we love, how we show appreciation, how we pray, how we treat others, how we get mad, how we rejoice, how we laugh . . .

I saw a funny post online that talked about how hard it is to "parent" the "you" out of your child. That can hit home fast, right? When we see our kids get upset over things just as we do or act just like us, it can be scary—but also eye-opening. The way we treat them is how they'll treat others . . . The way we handle circumstances, they'll learn from us. Even how they talk to their siblings reflects how we talk to them. When we realize they're looking up to us, their mama, their guiding light. . . we know to try our best each day to set a good example. I always say we must have grace and patience with others and ourselves.

As you talk to your children, you may hear your own

parents' words come out! Of course, there may be some things you catch yourself doing that you *do* want to pass along, and there are likely some things that should stop with you. Remember, Mama, no one is perfect. Just as you're trying your best, your parents did their best too, as did their parents before them. We all come from different backgrounds and upbringings. But with God's help, you can pass along the good things from yours to the next generation.

Remember, Mama, you can always come to God with prayer and thanks, no matter the circumstance, as we're reminded in I Thessalonians 5. He is here for you along your journey as a mom, and He will help guide you along the way!

 *Mama, what is it about yourself that you wish your kids would continue in their own lives? What do you wish you could change a bit and not see your children propagate? Each of us is a product of the things we have experienced and mixed with our personalities as nature and nurture come into play. Today, be a fly on the wall as you do life with your kids, taking note of how you react and how you behave around them. It will take some soul-searching, but, Mama, you have so many great things to give—let's bring them out!*

Not a Vacation

"Peace I leave with you; my peace I give to you.
Not as the world gives do I give to you.
Let not your hearts be troubled,
neither let them be afraid."

JOHN 14:27

When I was a kid, going on vacation was always such a fun time! I loved going to the ocean and collecting seashells. It wasn't until I took my own kids on our first vacation to the beach that I realized what my parents went through—and for them, it was not fully a vacation. Parents have to make sure everything the family needs for the week is packed, endure the whines of "When will we get there?" handle siblings fighting—it's a lot of stress, sometimes more than just being at home. When you're a mom, you don't get a vacation when you're on vacation.

But in John 14:27, Jesus says He is giving us peace. So where is this peace in the hustle and bustle of a family road trip, you ask? As moms, don't we need time for rest and relaxation too? If we are too stressed or busy to enjoy the time with our families, why are we even going? The truth is, we can find God's peace even on the busiest days of our lives. The peace He gives us is not the kind that comes with a dimly lit, quiet room, complete with relaxing music and rain sounds. No, we can ask God for His peace to stay with us through the packing of the van, the gas station stops, the unavoidable spills, and the traffic. Ask Him to give you peace of heart through all of it—give you the peace that only He can give. And then, my friends, take a deep breath, put on your seat belt, and enjoy the ride.

It's important to note that these times with all the kids on vacation are short-lived. They say you get around eighteen summers with them—which isn't much—before they're off and away in their own lives. So, Mama, try not to let the stresses of the day outweigh the experiences you'll have as you build family memories.

 *Maybe heading out to a beach destination is far from your immediate plans, but did you know that you can give your mind a vacation from where you are at this very moment? Take a moment to meditate on John 14 and receive the peace that God promises you today and always!*

In the Thick of It

Look carefully then how you walk,
not as unwise but as wise,
making the best use of the time,
because the days are evil.

EPHESIANS 5:15–16

We've all been there—it's been a long and tiring day, the kids are screaming, the food is burning, fifty things are left on the to-do list, and all you can hear is "Mom! Mommy! Mama!" You just want to lock yourself in the closet with some chocolate . . . I've been there too! Take a deep breath. This too shall pass—it will. There will be a time when the house is quiet. There will no longer be the pitter-patter of little feet or the calling for "Mom!" from across the house, and the laundry basket will be much less full. When the day gets crazy, try to put the craziness into perspective. Whether you believe it now or not, there will be a day when you will miss the chaos. And on that day, you are going to wish for just an hour back from when your kiddos were little. Pretend this is the hour you get back. What do you need to say that you didn't say? What do you want to do that you didn't get to do? What do you miss the most? Why not drop everything on your list and do that thing now?

I know it's hard to embrace the mess today and to be thankful for this craziness. You may be in the thick of it now, but the chaos will calm in time. As we're reminded in Ephesians, make the best use of this time now. Soak it all in, for tomorrow they'll be a day older—and you will too.

Mama, there will be days of chaos and days of calm (just kidding, it'll probably still be chaos!), but I'm there with you. Even as my children are growing older, I miss them when they were younger, so I get it. I feel for my parents, who are now grandparents, as they probably miss when I was younger too. Let's not wish the days away but instead enjoy each moment in the journey. Make the best use of the time you have today!

Accepting Who You Are

But now, O LORD, you are our Father;
we are the clay, and you are our potter;
we are all the work of your hand.

ISAIAH 64:8

Mama, you were fearfully and wonderfully made! Sometimes we can be so hard on ourselves, but I'm here to remind you that you are doing your best, you are beautiful, you are perfect just the way God made you, and you are worthy! The big question is: Have you accepted *you*, faults and all? We can criticize ourselves a lot, even daily, whether it's about how we look or what we do, and we bring ourselves down. Today, Mama, let's make a change to build ourselves up and give ourselves grace. We need to stop with the daily scrutiny and negative self-talk. If you think you'll never be good enough or that you just don't compare to everyone else, halt that thought right there. God doesn't make mistakes, and you were wonderfully made by the Master Potter!

Everyone has been made differently—with different likes, dislikes, talents, things we love, and things we would rather pass on. If we were all the same, the world would be pretty boring! Each of us has special things we're good at, talents that are unique to us. Mama, embrace that fact! It's okay if you're not the best cook or if you don't like the things others do—that's not you, and that's beautiful. Double down on your strengths and see how you can put those out into the world to further the kingdom of God. You have a beautiful purpose for your life—in fact, many purposes. The next time you hear that voice inside telling you you're not good enough, stop it in its tracks. Replace it with something positive. Celebrate the talents you've been blessed with and honor the One who gave them to you!

Mama, what are you good at? What do you love doing? How can you serve others or bring that gift out into the world? Sometimes it's the things we do at our jobs each day that we're best at, or maybe it's a hobby, or better yet, maybe it's yet to be discovered! Maybe you're excellent at wrapping gifts or hosting parties, or baking, or drawing, or saving for the future—the possibilities are endless—but there is so much to you that the world needs. Today, think of those things and give the glory to the One who gave those gifts to you!

Let God Plan

"For I know the plans I have for you,"
declares the LORD, "plans for welfare
and not for evil, to give you a future and a hope."

JEREMIAH 29:11

Are you a planner? Often, we need our day-planners to keep our schedules straight and write down *all the things*. Sometimes we even plan for our kids—they'll go to this college, be married by the age of twenty-five . . . And then the plans get derailed . . . They switch schools or they don't meet their spouse or they decide not to go to college or get married at all! Our thoughts of the "perfect way things should go" are shattered. What we forget is that we can plan all we want, but only God's plans will prevail. We can jump at first opportunities or take the "safest boat," but that boat may not last for the long haul. We need to realize God is working not only in our lives but in everyone else's too. What you are doing, even if you don't realize it right now, is all part of His greater plan. We can think we've gone down the wrong paths, and we may have, but God is with us the whole way, and He can weave everything into our stories and His greater purposes.

True joy comes when we soak up what God has for us in each moment, in each way throughout our lives. We may not know why we're in the season we're in, but it's for a reason. We must let go of our plans and hold tight to His, putting our faith and trust in Him, and in Him alone, rather than our earthly hopes and plans. Surrendering our plans to Him is hard, but that's where faith and trust come in. He works in His timing too, not ours. So, be patient, Mama, He's got it all figured out—we just have to trust and keep saying yes to the calling He has for our lives, then teach our children to do the same.

Mama, if you're anything like me, giving up control is hard. But who better to be in control and driving the ship than the Creator of the universe? He sees things we can't, and we need to remember that—both into the future and into the past. He's got it figured out, even when all we see is a mess. Today, choose to surrender your plans for His. Put your faith and trust in Him in all circumstances. And know that He'll equip you along the way—you were made for this!

When God Is Silent

The Spirit of the LORD speaks by me;
his word is on my tongue.

II SAMUEL 23:2

Hearing from God can truly be a mystery sometimes. In the Bible we hear of times when angels appeared, but we don't hear much of that happening today. I'm sure each of us has a different way in which we hear from God. Mine is more like a second thought that often can come out of nowhere, especially when I'm walking or in the shower . . . it is truly something hard to explain. People can wonder, *Is that God or my subconscious?* When I get nudges from Him, they are unique, and they often take me off guard. Sometimes "nudges" from the Holy Spirit involve good things that take you out of your comfort zone, that make you take a leap of faith. It's in these times that God has you rely on your faith in Him to take the next step, as He guides you along the way. When we don't hear from God or when we're not sure what that's like, though, we can feel He's silent. In life we'll have peaks and valleys, but it doesn't mean He's stopped working. He works even when we are sleeping! If you're in a quiet season, pray. Even if you can't hear Him, know He's there. Mama, don't lose hope or stop being encouraged in the dry seasons of life. The Living Water is still there and flowing . . .

He's never too busy for you, and He wants you to come to Him. If you're unsure of what to do next, open His Word. I recall many times when I was younger, I would open my Bible to just the word I needed, so give it a go! You never know what Scripture is waiting to encourage you for what you'll face today. Remember, it's His Word—the Word of God—and so if it seems He's silent, give it a try. You'll find He's right there, waiting for you.

Mama, what does it look like when God talks to you? How do you hear Him most often? How can you continue to build your relationship with Him and put your faith and trust in Him? Opening the Bible is a great way to draw closer to Him. If you're scared, worried, questioning, nervous, happy, or excited, come to Him in prayer—He wants to hear from you. You are loved, Mama, and God is working all things out for you.

Discipline

Fathers, do not provoke your children to anger,
but bring them up in the discipline
and instruction of the Lord.

EPHESIANS 6:4

Discipline is a hard topic, and I'm not here to tell you what's right or wrong, as each family and each child is different. However, some truth can be found in the book of Ephesians—to not provoke our children to anger but to discipline them in the instruction of the Lord. Now having three kids, I can see how each one is different and how one child listens differently than another. We've tried it all in the area of discipline, and we are still learning. But one truth that we can rely on is to discipline them for *their* own good, not from *our* anger at them for disobeying us. Often, they are too young to process certain things, or they may not understand yet that what they did was a "no-no." Although what they do can make us very upset in the moment, looking at it for what it is a few days later helps us understand it does not matter as much in the long run. Taking a breath can certainly help. The Scriptures tell us this: "Whoever is slow to anger has great understanding, but he who has a hasty temper exalts folly" (Proverbs 14:29); "Know this, my beloved brothers: let every person be quick to hear, slow to speak, slow to anger" (James

1:19). These verses are great reminders for us—we're called to be slow to anger, listen to the situation, and discipline in love. How we react will live far beyond the moment in our child's heart. Instead, think before you speak, yell, or get upset. Did the child act on purpose, or was it an accident? Think about what you need to fix first. What lesson can be learned? Can you be gentle and encouraging yet firm? This is something we all can work on, and it may take some time. No one is perfect, not you and not your children, and that's why grace is so needed—for all of us!

Mama, I'm sure discipline happens in your home. I need to remind myself of these Scriptures to be slow to anger rather than get upset right away. We must extend grace to both ourselves and our children—and forgive them. Proverbs 19:11 is another great Scripture to be reminded of in these times: "Good sense makes one slow to anger, and it is his glory to overlook an offense." Each of us is learning every day, so, Mama, take it all in stride—you were made for this!

Wonder-fully Made

Having Grace

But by the grace of God I am what I am, and his grace toward me was not in vain. On the contrary, I worked harder than any of them, though it was not I, but the grace of God that is with me.

I CORINTHIANS 15:10

Mama, do you feel like you deserve grace each day? John 1:16 tells us this: "For from [Jesus's] fullness we have all received, grace upon grace." God extends His grace to you. Just as our Father in heaven extends grace to us, we should extend grace to our children. This is not a "get out of jail free" card, like we might draw in Monopoly, but rather, it's an extension of love, a gift. Giving grace is harder for some people than others. I'm sure there are times too when we wish others would extend grace to us—maybe it's when we're driving or when we forget something important. Maybe we even hope the other moms at the playground will extend grace to us when our kids are melting down. We need to remember that none of us is perfect. We are all sinners, and it's only by the grace of God that we are saved. Ask yourself today: As you react to things that happen to you, do you extend grace much or do you hold grudges? Are you quick to be judgmental or do you easily extend mercy? Today is a good day to look within your heart at how you react to other people, especially your children. When we show our kids grace, they learn from us, and then they extend grace to others. If you are experiencing negative feelings, give them to God and intentionally extend grace and forgiveness. You have enough on your mind as it is, Mama, so learn to let offense be like water flowing off a duck, as my grandma would say! Release that stress and negativity and replace it with grace and peace.

Mama, what does grace look like in your life? Do you need to extend more grace than you currently do? If God can give grace to you as a sinner, what's stopping you from extending that grace to your children or your neighbor or your child's teacher or coach? Today, look up a few Scriptures that discuss grace: II Corinthians 9:8; I Peter 5:10; and II Timothy 4:22. What can you learn from these verses and apply to your life?

Walk by Faith

And Jesus answered them, "Have faith in God.
Truly, I say to you, whoever says to this mountain,
'Be taken up and thrown into the sea,' and does not
doubt in his heart, but believes that what he says
will come to pass, it will be done for him.
Therefore I tell you, whatever you ask in prayer,
believe that you have received it, and it will be yours."

MARK 11:22–24

What does the word *faith* mean to you? Close your eyes, and picture yourself in a dark tunnel with Jesus beside you. You can't see Him, but you know He's there—or rather, you *have faith* that He's there . . . and so you keep walking forward, even when you can't see. You are trusting that He'll bring you to the light at the end of the tunnel. We are reminded of these words in II Corinthians 5:7: "For we walk by faith, not by sight." I don't know about you, but I would be frightened in that tunnel if I couldn't see! But that tunnel is a lot like life. When we pray, we need to have faith instead of doubt. As we go about life, we need to have faith and trust as we encounter each day that God will see us through. As our faith grows, so do our faith roots. It can be easy to fall into the trap of being anxious or worried, but God calls us to give Him our worries and replace them with faith. "Now faith is the assurance of things hoped for, the conviction of things not seen" (Hebrews 11:1). We're called many times to have faith in God and to push away any doubt. We're reminded in Ephesians 2:8–9: "For by grace you have been saved through faith. And this is not your own doing; it is the gift of God, not a result of works, so that no one may boast."

Mama, where are you in your faith journey? Many of us have faith but still cling to worry. Take note of this passage in Matthew 14:26–31: "When the disciples saw [Jesus] walking on the lake . . . 'Lord, if it's you,' Peter replied, 'tell me to come to you on the water.' 'Come,' he said. Then Peter got down out of the boat, walked on the water and came toward Jesus. But when he saw the wind, he was afraid and, beginning to sink, cried out, 'Lord, save me!' Immediately Jesus reached out his hand and caught him. 'You of little faith,' he said, 'why did you doubt?'" (NIV).

Seek Him First

"You will seek me and find me,
when you seek me with all your heart."

JEREMIAH 29:13

Many Scriptures in the Bible talk about seeking God—and they all talk about seeking Him with our hearts, calling on Him, and He will be near. Take a look at these verses: "Seek the LORD while he may be found; call upon him while he is near" (Isaiah 55:6); "Instead, seek his kingdom, and these things will be added to you" (Luke 12:31); "Therefore do not be anxious, saying, 'What shall we eat?' or 'What shall we drink?' or 'What shall we wear?' For the Gentiles seek after all these things, and your heavenly Father knows that you need them all. But seek first the kingdom of God and his righteousness, and all these things will be added to you" (Matthew 6:31–33).

We can rest assured that as we seek the kingdom of God, our needs will be fulfilled. God cares for us and our every need! If we seek fulfillment in earthly things, though, we're focused on the wrong prize. When we seek God and His plans for us, we will be fulfilled. We can do this in many ways: by acknowledging and thanking Him, by worshiping Him, by seeking Him for comfort, by pouring our hearts out to Him, and by trusting Him, even in the trials of life. When we learn to rely on Him over anyone else, we will grow faith and trust in Him and what He can do for us!

 *As busy moms, we are often living in our own states of triage—what needs done first and when, who needs what and when, what's most important right now and what can wait. We may try to find time with God, but it often gets put on the back burner. Did you know, Mama, that you can find ways through the chaos to still seek Him? You can do this by how you respond each day, how you live out your life, how you come to Him in thanks and praise, how you pray in the shower or the car . . . He knows you're busy, and He's there for you. Today, send up some thanks to Him for whatever you're grateful for. Where can you give Him the glory and praise Him today, even if you're in the middle of a storm?*

Mom Guilt

But he said to me, "My grace is sufficient for you,
for my power is made perfect in weakness."
Therefore I will boast all the more gladly
of my weaknesses, so that the power of Christ
may rest upon me.

II CORINTHIANS 12:9

I don't know about you, Mama, but I sometimes struggle with "mom guilt." Some days, no matter what I do—whether I go into the office or stay at home to work, or even at an appointment or away from my kids in any fashion—I feel guilty if I can't be with them. If you're like me, you're not alone in feeling that mom guilt. Mamas can feel guilty in so many ways—for working, for *not* working, for being at home, for *not* being at home, for not throwing the best party ever, for feeling like we failed at making dinner, and for not living up to the supermoms we see on social media. We put so much pressure on ourselves, and it really can eat at us. The feeling of guilt doesn't allow us to have peace inside.

Mama, you are doing the best you can. No one is perfect, and each family situation is different. Take heart in knowing that you are loved—both by your children and by the One Most High. He sees you, and He cares for you. We need to choose not to accept those feelings of guilt and instead replace them with truth. Guilt: *I didn't make a good dinner for my kids tonight because I was so busy . . .* Truth: *I'm glad my children are able to eat dinner tonight.* Guilt: *I have to leave my kids in the care of others so I can work.* Truth: *I am a great mom, and I'm providing for my family.*

Today's world is not the same as it was years ago, when the norm was for a mom to stay home. Most moms today have to work to provide for their families, and the guilt can pour in from that. If you're a working mama, let your children see how much you love them as you provide for them and give back to the world by using your God-given gifts and talents!

No matter what brings you the mom guilt, Mama, replace it with truth instead. Let's practice a few scenarios and see how you can turn that guilt into truth. What are a few ways that your mom guilt has set in, either currently or in the past? Let's rewrite them to find peace and acceptance instead. If you feel guilty for leaving to see your friends or doing something fun for yourself, I'm with you! Let's instead realize we have worth; we are more than just "Mom." You are (your name here)—a daughter of the King. Don't let your "mom" title define you; you are allowed to have fun and be, well, you!

Missed Opportunities

Don't compare yourself with others.
Just look at your own work to see
if you have done anything to be proud of.
You must each accept
the responsibilities that are yours.
GALATIANS 6:4-6 ERV

Have you ever heard your kids say, "My friend has one of these—so why can't I have it too?" or, "This person got accepted to . . . /made the team . . . /gets to do this . . . but I didn't!" Some kids are allowed to go places, do things—like have phones—or they get into certain groups or participate in activities your kids aren't in—and this can be hard on them. They start to feel like outsiders looking in.

Even at a young age, kids start to compare themselves to others and think, *Why not me?* They can start to feel unworthy and feel left out. Help them to understand they are not worth any less! They need to learn this lesson early, because they will face it throughout life, as they don't get into certain schools, don't get to date the boyfriend/girlfriend they liked, or face challenges with work, marriage, and their own kids and friends.

We all should take note of Galatians 6 and look into our own lives, our own work, to see what we can be proud of for ourselves. We can replace the negative feelings concerning missed opportunities with a blessing or a truth that we see in our lives. There is even more guidance from I Samuel 16:7: "For the LORD sees not as man sees: man looks on the outward appearance, but the Lord looks on the heart.'" So much of our comparison is of earthly things or treasures, when we should be working to store our treasures in heaven. Help your children count their blessings instead of focusing on what they've missed out on and find other reasons to be joyful. A missed opportunity just means God has something better planned!

Mama, it's hard not to compare ourselves to others and feel like we're missing out . . . and our kids are beginning to realize this too. They often want to be just like their friends. In the world of social media too, the fear of missing out can be strong. It happens to all of us. Instead of focusing on those things that cause us to lose joy, focus on blessings. There are probably many things you have today that you longed for in the past. Don't give a negative situation power over your happiness!

Losing Yourself

And he said to them, "Come away by yourselves
to a desolate place and rest a while."
For many were coming and going,
and they had no leisure even to eat.

MARK 6:31

It's easy to lose ourselves in the "mom title." It used to take me a long time to get ready in the morning—but that time is now lowered to about fifteen minutes. I have, on more than one occasion, forgotten when I washed my hair last! Many things I used to love—like getting together with my friends or watching what I love to watch on TV—just don't happen as often as they used to. Usually, kids' shows are now on the TV, and my days are jam-packed between work, life, and kids.

Maybe you're in the same season as me—when you start to lose yourself and the things you used to have time to do because you're so busy being a mom. But, Mama, there were probably days when you were being you, *before* kids, when you longed for the days you're in now. It's up to us to find a good balance between the mom life and remembering who we were and what we loved doing before being "mom."

Mom life can be exhausting in multiple ways. Sometimes having a girls' night out or doing something just for yourself (maybe a Target run?) can recharge our batteries. Mark 6 shows us that Jesus understands the need to get away and rejuvenate. And God is with us in that rest . . . He knows we need to recharge our batteries. If we don't show ourselves love, it will become harder to love others. Mama, it's okay to step away from your duties for a bit; you'll come back ready to better serve your children and families after you've had a little rest!

Mama, I too struggle with the guilt of stepping away to do something just for me—even if that's just taking a walk or running to the store. Often our batteries can be drained by the responsibilities we face all day long, and it's okay for your children to have some fun when you're not around too. Finding a great sitter (who has some energy!) and planning a night out can let your soul recharge a bit. What do rest, recharging, and finding yourself look like for you? Mama, plan some time soon to step away and get the rejuvenation you need and deserve!

The Enemy

Submit yourselves therefore to God.
Resist the devil, and he will flee from you.

JAMES 4:7

What causes you to stress or worry? What lies do you tell yourself that you have learned to believe? What problems does your mind keep rehearsing that keep you feeling anxious? We often hold on to these lies as truths, and they make us scared, upset, sad, worried, and *stressed*! The evil one knows what will make you upset, and he will bombard you with untruths until you start to begin to believe them—and even the smallest of his lies cause damage. They can build up and draw you further from God and His plans and purpose for you. They can steal your joy. These lies can tear apart marriages, relationships, jobs, goals, dreams, and much more.

I was at a worship service recently, and while I was singing worship songs to the Lord, the enemy began attacking me, trying to draw me away from my time with the Lord. If I had focused on his lies rather than on the Lord, I might have been dragged down, but I stopped and realized what was going on. When the lies start pouring in, call out to Jesus. Repeat the Lord's Prayer or another favorite Scripture and fill your mind with good things. Trust in God, not in the lies, and set your heart to pray. When negative thoughts come in from the enemy, ask yourself: *Is this of God? Why would He say these things about someone He made and has a beautiful purpose for (me!)?* Don't believe the enemy, but instead turn toward the light. When you resist the devil, he has to leave!

You can stand against the enemy by putting on the armor of God: "Therefore put on the full armor of God, so that when the day of evil comes, you may be able to stand your ground, and after you have done everything, to stand. Stand firm then, with the belt of truth buckled around your waist, with the breastplate of righteousness in place, and with your feet fitted with the readiness that comes from the gospel of peace. In addition to all this, take up the shield of faith, with which you can extinguish all the flaming arrows of the evil one. Take the helmet of salvation and the sword of the Spirit, which is the word of God. And pray in the Spirit on all occasions with all kinds of prayers and requests. With this in mind, be alert and always keep on praying for all the Lord's people" (Ephesians 6:13–18 NIV).

God Is Your Refuge

God is our refuge and strength. . . .
God is within her, she will not fall.

PSALM 46:1, 5 NIV

Mama, take a look within your heart and soul—how are you? When daily stresses and storms arise, we can listen to the enemy and believe his lies, for he will make mountains out of molehills and sweep storms into our souls made up of worries and anxiety. If we believe these lies, our hearts will be stripped of joy, and the enemy will win. If God is love and light, then the enemy is hatred and darkness. There will always be hard times and troubles, worries and stress. Thankfully, we can seek rest and shelter in the Lord, for He is our refuge and strength.

Psalm 31:3–5 gives us a great reminder: "You [God] are my refuge and defense; guide me and lead me as you have promised. Keep me safe from the trap that has been set for me; shelter me from danger. I place myself in your care. You will save me, LORD; you are a faithful God" (GNT). God wants us to seek Him first and give all our cares to Him, for He will fight for us. We can find shelter—a warm, loving place—when we seek the Lord during our storms. We must remember He brings us joy! He wants us to enjoy this beautiful life and earth that have been given to us, while the enemy is out for our destruction. We can come to God at any time, for anything.

Deuteronomy 33:27 brings such a powerful truth: "The eternal God is your dwelling place, and underneath are the everlasting arms." When you are weak, God is strong. When you need a loving embrace, His arms are wide open for you. When you need someone to hold you up, He will carry you. He is your refuge and strength!

Mama, when you pour your heart out, Jesus is there, listening, and He loves you! Let Him be your refuge. No matter what you're battling, including the lies that cause you to worry or fear, run to the arms of Jesus. Find love, light, hope, and warmth in Him!

Worry Finder or Hope Seeker?

Rejoice in hope, be patient in tribulation,
be constant in prayer.
ROMANS 12:12

How would you answer this age-old question: Do you see the cup as half-full or half-empty? When you face each day, you should ask yourself this: Am I focusing on what could possibly go wrong or am I focusing on all the good that surrounds me?

We're reminded in Romans 12:12 to do three things:

1. Rejoice in hope, meaning to find joy, happiness, or a sense of gladness in the expectation of positive things to come.

2. Be patient in tribulation, meaning to remain positive in the face of challenges.

3. Be constant in prayer, meaning to have a consistent and persistent dialogue with God.

While these three instructions seem easy enough on the average day, it's a little harder to follow through when life is hard. After all, when we are grieving a loss or having health concerns or wondering how we are going to afford our utility bills next month, it's not easy to concentrate on rejoicing or being patient or even being in constant communication with God. When you find yourself in one of these painful situations where you just can't look past it to see any hope, look to Scripture to find what God says is the best course of action. Psalm 33: 20-22 (NLT) says "We put our hope in the Lord. He is our help and our shield." James 1:2-3 says "Count it all joy . . . when you meet trials of various kinds, for you know that the testing of your faith produces steadfastness." Philippians 4:6 says "Do not be anxious about anything, but in everything by prayer . . . let your requests be made known to God."

Over and over again, the Bible tells us to rejoice, to remain steadfast, and to pray without ceasing. So, even when the road is tough, keep your head up, Mama. Lean on the promises of God, find strength in His words, and trust that, despite the challenges, there is hope in Him. There is goodness in today that is worth focusing on. Find it, hold on to it, and let it lighten your heart.

 *Today, Mama, test your own faith. What is bothering you today? It could be anything from something at home to work to life in general. Whatever it is, bring it to God—and then leave it there, wholeheartedly. Then have faith and simply wait. Sometimes it can take days, months, or years . . . but know He's working on the problem, for His plan and His glory.*

Beautiful girl, you can do hard things.

Chaos Coordinator

"Fear not, for I am with you;
be not dismayed, for I am your God;
I will strengthen you, I will help you,
I will uphold you with my righteous right hand."

ISAIAH 41:10

Mama, you are seen by the One Most High. As chaos swarms around you as a busy mom, God wants to remind you that He is with you and He will strengthen and help you! These words are so beautiful to hear, especially when the world is swirling around you.

Mama, there will be moments of chaos, but just like with all raging seas, the calm will return. Still, when you're about to lose your cool, take a step back and breathe for a few moments . . . Remember, this time won't last forever. When your children have made a huge mess and you are about to respond in an ungodly way, stop and think first. Is this really a discipline moment, or are you just upset? If your child were you as a little girl, how would you have wanted your own mom to respond? Would you have wanted her to join in the chaos with you and put aside wanting to keep things neat and tidy? Would you want her to give you the biggest hug and let you know it was all going to be okay? Would you want her to distract you with a game while you wait for your food to come to the table (hello, I Spy!)? Or is there a lesson to be learned?

Remember, God wants us to be slow to anger and give grace, just as He's given to us. Let God fill you with peace today, and don't let your anger take over the moment. Practice patience and love!

Mama, we all have times of chaos. And there are all types of chaos—especially since what can annoy us the most is often the most fun to our children! We have to let them be kids at times—and sometimes we should even join in on the fun. The moment will soon be gone, but the memories will last. If you're at your wits' end, pray and ask the Lord for help. He will give you the strength you need to get through the daily chaos and challenges. Being a mom is not easy, but God is with you. You got this, Mama!

One Day at a Time

"Therefore do not be anxious about tomorrow,
for tomorrow will be anxious for itself.
Sufficient for the day is its own trouble."

MATTHEW 6:34

For us mamas, each day can bring its own challenges. Jesus told us this in Matthew 6, that each day can bring its own trouble, but we're called to not worry about it. It's hard to not do this, especially when we care so deeply for our children. How are we supposed to not worry or be anxious when she has a high fever today and we're sure her condition will only get worse tomorrow? How are we supposed to not worry or be anxious when he has worked so hard to be on the team and he finds out tomorrow if he is going to make it? How are we supposed to not worry or be anxious when we went negative in our checking account today and we don't have any lunch money to give the kids tomorrow?

God says that worrying about tomorrow's problems simply don't help anything. So today, let's concentrate on the fever she has now, not how it might get worse. Let's concentrate on telling him how proud he should be of himself for working so hard at something he wants, not on the heartbreak he might get tomorrow. Let's concentrate on how to get back in good standing with the bank, not on the possibility that the kids will go without lunch tomorrow (God is going before you. He will work it out.).

Let's be reminded today that God holds all our tomorrows. He is working out His plans for us even as we sleep. On those days when you feel overwhelmed by troubles, Mama, take it one day at a time. There's enough going on today that requires your focus—trust that tomorrow will be a brand-new day. It helps when we go to bed to know that the day will be new in the morning. As my dad used to say, the sun may not always shine, but it will always come up!

 Just as Jesus reminds us in Matthew 6, God will take care of our needs. We don't have to be anxious about each new day. Instead, we must turn our face toward Jesus, leaving the toils of each day behind us. Mama, take a look at your days—are they full of anxious thoughts or grace-filled moments? Trust me, I need this reminder daily too, so Mama, you are not alone. When you find yourself in those moments of stress and chaos, be reminded of these passages. They will bring you peace and strength to take on each new day!

God Loves Them

But when Jesus saw it,
he was indignant and said to them,
"Let the children come to me; do not hinder them,
for to such belongs the kingdom of God."

MARK 10:14

When I grew up in Sunday school, we used to sing this song: "Jesus loves the little children, all the children of the world . . ." Even at a young age, I knew that Jesus loves *all of us*—and that includes our children too. He has so many great purposes for their lives, and He has given them such beautiful gifts and talents. We must always remember that God's plans for their lives aren't always what we want for them, so when they lose friends or choose a different career path, let God work it out. He is there with them, even when we can't see or understand what is happening. He is creating them to be who they were made to be. That means they'll face trials and they'll go through challenges along the way. These times can break us as mamas, as we try to shield them from any pain, but instead, we need to view these times as testimonies and realize that God is working through them— we may not understand it now, but we may in time. We just have to have faith and trust Him.

It may be harder for your kids to understand this, but

as you teach them about Jesus and help them grow in their faith, they will learn to understand. God will work out His plan in their lives because He loves them. Keep setting a good example and being faithful yourself, Mama—your kids are watching you!

Mama, soak up the love, joy, peace of the Lord, knowing that God loves your children even more than you do. He loves how unique each one is, and He has given them such different and unique gifts and talents. Today, let's end our devotion in a prayer: God, thank You for my children. Thank You for making each one in Your image, perfectly unique. Lord, stay beside them in their own faith journeys and help them to know that You are Lord of all. Help them to realize in their trials that You have something better planned, that You have written a beautiful story and have an amazing purpose for them. Help me to have strength each day to be there for them and love them as You would. I pray these things in Jesus's name, amen.

Helpful

*In all things I have shown you that by working hard
in this way we must help the weak and remember
the words of the Lord Jesus, how he himself said,
"It is more blessed to give than to receive."*

ACTS 20:35

Isn't it a blessing when your children are helpful? Mine are now getting to the age when they'll put their dishes in the sink after dinner and help clean up. Mama, getting help from them is like taking a deep breath of fresh air! Teaching them to help out at home translates to good behavior when they're at school, at a neighbor's house, and beyond. Always tell them how thankful you are for their help and how it made you feel. This teaches them that their help has a beautiful effect on others. Teaching responsibility can help alleviate you of feeling like you have to do it all, as well. You can start small, like having them clean up their own toys or help with fun chores around the house. My kids even love picking up sticks in our backyard—it helps us and it helps them see the value of hard work too!

We learn from Acts 20 that it is better to give than receive. How can you extend this helpfulness beyond your front door? How can your children help a neighbor or the community in which you live? This summer, a few kids on our block handed out free lemonade to the community—without asking for anything in return, simply to quench the thirst of anyone who walked by. Your kids might decide to rake leaves for a neighbor or hold the door open for someone at the store. As they experience the appreciation of others, it will warm their hearts.

I really like the words of Hebrews 13:16: "Do not neglect to do good and to share what you have, for such sacrifices are pleasing to God."

Mama, you have a helper on hand. Maybe your little one is too young or maybe your teenager has already moved out of the house, but you can still encourage them to be genuinely helpful to others. We can teach our kids, no matter their age, to never be helpful reluctantly or with a sour heart but to genuinely show kindness to others and do it to give glory to God. When others see us acting like Jesus would, they may even pass it on to others. You never know whose day might be improved, and there's no day better to start than now!

Saying No

"Let what you say be simply 'Yes' or 'No';
anything more than this comes from evil."
MATTHEW 5:37

Mama, is it easy or hard for you to say no? It's probably easier to say no to our kids than to turn down a request from a friend or coworker. We usually don't want to upset other people. Sometimes our kids will push back against us or get upset when we tell them they can't do something, but we know our answer is for their own good. Did you know we need to parent ourselves sometimes too? We can end up taking on too much, and our plates get overly full. We say "yes" to requests such as helping out in sports leagues, being homeroom moms, and hosting playdates . . . Our schedules can get so full that we have no time for rest.

Mama, you are allowed to say no to events, meetings, and activities that aren't good fits for you, whether it doesn't work because you already have something scheduled or it doesn't work because you don't have the energy or emotional capacity to take it on. Some of us love to be busy, while others find an eventful lifestyle to be draining. Either way, when there is no room for quality time with your immediate family, let alone your extended family and close friends, it can take a toll on you. If you find yourself constantly looking forward to any spare moment you can get, it's probably time to reevaluate your schedule of events.

We live in a go-go-go society, and the fear of missing out or disappointing someone can be very real. Next time you are asked to volunteer your time and energy, ask God if this is something He wants you to do, and whether the answer is *yes* or *no*, you can feel good knowing that you followed God's lead.

Mama, take a look at everything you are taking on, what you are saying yes to inside and outside your house. What things have you and/or your kids signed up for—and is it bringing on more or less stress? This week, see where you can take better charge of your schedule and find some time to rest before taking on the next thing. Don't be afraid to say no and see how lightening up on a few things can help add more stress-free moments to your day.

Parenting Together

Do not be unequally yoked with unbelievers.
For what partnership has righteousness
with lawlessness? Or what fellowship
has light with darkness?

II CORINTHIANS 6:14

Setting rules and boundaries for our children takes more than just us. I'm sure there've been times when you or your husband has said no to something and the kids went to ask the other parent instead, or when values/actions haven't been aligned between you and your spouse. It's hard when this happens, but II Corinthians 6 tells us we must be in line with one another—and that includes all those who are parenting your children, from you and your spouse to their grandparents and all those who watch your children.

Getting on the same page about what's allowed and what's not will help your children, as the parenting will be consistent across the board. The best way to make that happen is by talking together to come up with a good plan. There can be boundaries and house rules—even written down on the family bulletin board—so there is no question. It's hard if both parents aren't aligned spiritually, but this frequently happens in families. When you don't have the same values, morals, and beliefs as your spouse, it can seem as if you're pushing and pulling each other in your relationship. If anything is in question, though, you can always go to God's Word, which is always the best tiebreaker.

When it comes down to it, everyone should be most concerned about the good of the children, and that's what we all should remember at the end of the day. Compromise can be a good thing too, and new traditions can be formed as we keep others alive. No matter what, if everyone loves the children, you can find a way to help them grow up well!

Mama, do you see eye to eye with your husband when it comes to parenting? In what areas are you not aligned? This week, take a good look at any potential gaps in your parenting. Are there any new rules that need to be established, or does anything need to be changed as your children grow? Don't worry, Mama, we're all in this together, and we all have challenges when it comes to parenting. As II Corinthians tells us, we can learn to be equally yoked, no matter how tough it is. Remember, Mama, you were made for this!

Allowed to Be Happy

Delight yourself in the LORD, and he will give you the
desires of your heart. Commit your way to the LORD;
trust in him, and he will act.

PSALM 37:4–5

Hey you, yes you (the amazing woman reading this book)—you're allowed to be happy! First Thessalonians 5:16–18 reminds us to "rejoice always, pray without ceasing, give thanks in all circumstances; for this is the will of God in Christ Jesus for you." In anything and everything—in the good times and the bad—you can rejoice! One way is to look past your current circumstances to the purpose on the other side of them. God doesn't put anything in your path that He doesn't use to grow and strengthen you. Today may be hard, but tomorrow you will have gained wisdom, perseverance, empathy, and courage—characteristics that will only help you on this motherhood journey.

Plus, on the other side of this difficulty, you will be better suited to help others by sharing how God used your circumstances for good—for His glory, to teach you and rescue you. Sometimes God even purposely places people on your path because He needs you to give them a message. Be sure to follow God's nudges when it comes to who will benefit from you sharing, though. Our little ones are not equipped emotionally or mentally to take on adult situations. And if you feel as if you need help processing your pain, there is nothing wrong with seeking professional counseling services.

If you have a hard time being happy, Mama, I am with you. Some days my negative thoughts are so loud they seem to take over; while other days I'm able to turn up the volume on my positive thoughts so they become louder than my anxiety and stress. If you are having one of those rough, loud-negative-thought days, know this: You can place anything at His feet; He will help you to carry whatever is stealing your joy; He has an amazing plan for your life; and He wants you to enjoy this world.

If you are just a happy person in general, praise the Lord! Embrace it! If you naturally have a pessimistic outlook, maybe it's time to step away from the person, place, or situation that's stealing your joy, and change your scenery—it's okay to take a break from daily life now and then to focus on your happiness. Today, come to the Lord with all that's on your heart and offload any worries or concerns. Let Him work it all out while you focus on maintaining your peace and joy!

People-Pleasing

For am I now seeking the approval of man,
or of God? Or am I trying to please man?
If I were still trying to please man,
I would not be a servant of Christ.

GALATIANS 1:10

So many times, we moms focus on pleasing others, putting our own needs in the back seat. We are reminded in Galatians 1 to not look to please man but rather to focus on serving the Lord. Consider how you might be trying to people-please. Are you one of those who is always saying yes and always putting others first? Do you avoid conflict and apologize excessively? Do you fear rejection and criticism? Do you take on more burdens or responsibilities than you could ever possibly manage? If you answered yes to any of these questions, you might be more focused on pleasing people than you are on pleasing God. Set some time to set your priorities—what actions do you need to take to grow closer in your relationship with God? And then establish clear boundaries. If someone is asking you to volunteer or run an errand or give them a ride, ask yourself: is this action a priority that is pleasing to God? Is this action going to help me grow closer to Him?

We are to speak, eat, work, live, and act in ways that are

meant to bring glory to God and not to please men. People-pleasing is a hard trap to escape, but if we can free ourselves from it, we can say no more freely to things we don't need to be doing, and we can be happy without worrying what others will think. Mama, start focusing your attention on God rather than on other people's expectations of you. It won't be an overnight process to avoid the people-pleasing trap, but as you begin to catch yourself doing it, realize your worth is great in God's eyes, and you don't have to sacrifice your own needs to please others.

Mama, what does people-pleasing look like for you? Do you ever look at it from a "people-pleasing versus God-pleasing" perspective? What changes do you need to make in your life in this area? Let's end today in prayer: Lord, help me to have the strength to please You first and stand up for myself instead of falling into the trap of pleasing others. Help me to seek Your will over that of other people. Lord, I pray that You would guide me in all the decisions of my life so I can live out the purpose You have for me and my family. I ask these things in Jesus's name, amen.

Suffering

And he withdrew from them about a stone's throw,
and knelt down and prayed, saying, "Father, if you are
willing, remove this cup from me. Nevertheless, not my
will, but yours, be done." And there appeared to him
an angel from heaven, strengthening him.

LUKE 22:41-43

All of us experience suffering in life. We each experience loss and pain in one way or another. The night before Jesus was tortured and crucified, He knew what awaited Him the next day. And even though Jesus prayed to God the Father to take away the suffering that Jesus was about to endure, it was more important to Jesus that God's will be done than it was for Jesus to take the easy way out. Also, we learn in the Lord's Prayer, "Thy will be done, on earth as it is in heaven."

Are you in alignment with God's plan for your life? Is He a part of your decision-making process? There is no better feeling than when you know that He is guiding your steps, because even though it might be a hard step to take, you are taking it with fearless confidence and a heart full of contentment. That doesn't mean that we won't suffer. Rather, God meets us where we are in the midst of our suffering—and we are reminded that He is there with us.

Even in times of sadness, the Lord never leaves us nor

forsakes us. As I Peter 4:19 says: "Therefore let those who suffer according to God's will entrust their souls to a faithful Creator while doing good." As we follow this instruction, the trials we go through can make us stronger, causing our faith roots to grow deep. Just as a tree with weak roots can fall during a storm, a weak faith in Christ could falter during a difficult challenge if we do not strengthen our roots as believers in Him.

When trials happen, Mama, hold strong in your faith and trust in the Lord; do not let yourself be easily shaken. The storms will come, but we know God's will and plans are much better than ours—and He is always in control!

 *When you go out with very young children, Mama, don't you always pack whatever you think you might need? You take along juice boxes, snacks, wet wipes, maybe even some first-aid items. You're ready for it all! Mama, sometimes we need our own "care kits" so we can be ready when trials come. Each time you experience suffering, you can gain endurance, character, and hope if you turn toward Jesus in the situation. Remember that God is working in and through all things, not just for you but for everyone else too. Stay strong, Mama!*

Even when you don't feel it, He's working.

Jesus's Lineage

Therefore the Lord himself will give you a sign.
Behold, the virgin shall conceive and bear a son,
and shall call his name Immanuel.

ISAIAH 7:14

I don't know about you, but reading the genealogy lists in the Bible is something I tend to skip over. What's amazing, though, is that God has used some amazing women as a part of Jesus's lineage and story. Tamar is one of the first. After her first two husbands died, according to the Law, she was to marry the third son of Judah, but when she realized he wasn't going to let that happen, she tricked Judah into having relations with her—and she became pregnant. Her story is full of loss and betrayal.

Rahab was a Gentile and a prostitute who negotiated with the Israelite spies to save her family when they were taking the Promised Land. Next is Ruth. Naomi and her family moved to Moab because there was not enough food in Israel, but then Naomi's husband died. Her son had married a Moabite woman, Ruth, but in time, her husband also passed away. Ruth and Naomi were both widows, but Ruth was committed to caring for her mother-in-law. When they heard Naomi's homeland had crops, they moved back. Naomi's relative Boaz owned fields there, and he ended up marrying Ruth; they had a son, who became the grandfather of King David.

Bathsheba was the wife of Uriah, yet she had relations with King David. When she became pregnant, David had her husband killed. David eventually repented, and God granted them a son. Bathsheba later became the mother of King Solomon.

Finally, God had favor on Mary, a virgin who was godly but not sinless. She was entrusted to carry God's only Son, Jesus, while she was still betrothed to Joseph.

Each of these extraordinary women became mothers, despite pasts filled with sin and hardship. Jesus's lineage gives us hope and shows that no matter our past, we can make a change and decide to follow Jesus and His plans for our lives.

Mama, how amazing is it that these women were the great-great-grandmothers of Jesus! We can see from their stories that even when things look bleak and when we don't see how God can ever come through, He does—in extraordinary ways. You are a part of not only your own story but the stories of those who come after you and after them—it will go on and on!

Passing It On

Children, obey your parents in everything,
for this pleases the Lord.

COLOSSIANS 3:20

Being a mom is a grand blessing and an incredible opportunity. It's amazing to see what kinds of things our children inherit from us. Maybe even now you see characteristics of your husband or yourself in your children. We are entrusted with the responsibility of raising our children—and raising them as well as we can. All parents pass on certain traits—both good and bad—to their kids.

Our children don't just get genetic characteristics from us—they also learn from us many other things, including ways to handle situations. It's up to us to teach our children how to become who they are meant to be. Mama, look to the Scriptures to see how to instill godly traits in your kids, traits such as being slow to anger, loving their neighbors, not judging others, helping one another, showing love, care, and compassion, honoring their father and mother, turning from sin, following the Lord, giving all their worries to Him, and trusting His plans for their lives—along with many other things too.

We must help guide them in this journey as they learn the ways of God—it's up to us to lead them on the right paths.

Mama, this is not an easy task or one to be taken lightly, but you were made for this! God planned for you to be their mama, and that is a beautiful blessing! When you are weak, let God give you His strength. There will be days filled with mistakes, days when you want to run for the hills, but this is all a part of the journey. Keep doing what you can—and remember that God is there as your refuge whenever you need guidance or a listening ear!

Mama, it is such a great privilege to help shape the next generation. Just know that you are never walking this journey alone. Each mom has her own struggles, and she is doing what she can do each day. Whenever you need help and guidance, just pray. God already knows your heart, and He's walking with you each day. Mama, raising amazing kids is worth all the sacrifices you'll make. It's a tough journey, but you have mama strength, and you've got this!

Giving Other Moms Grace

Love does no wrong to a neighbor;
therefore love is the fulfilling of the law.

ROMANS 13:10

Mama, it's time for some honest talk. Have you ever judged another mom? Maybe a better question is: In what ways did you judge her? Even a quick critique of what she's wearing to the bus stop or how her kids are behaving can count as judgment. At times we consider ourselves as more "put together" or better moms in comparison, but why do we do this?

I like the reminder found in Romans 2:1–3: "Therefore you have no excuse, O man, every one of you who judges. For in passing judgment on another you condemn yourself, because you, the judge, practice the very same things. We know that the judgment of God rightly falls on those who practice such things. Do you suppose, O man—you who judge those who practice such things and yet do them yourself—that you will escape the judgment of God?"

Mama, when you step out of the house to go somewhere and you don't have on your makeup or time to do your hair, do you ever think, *I hope they don't judge me?* One hot day, my daughter was sweating, and I told her I could put her hair up, and for once, she agreed that I could. But after I finished, she said, "Mom, I really hope no one sees me!" Now, she is just four years old! My husband and I laughed at her wit, but can you see that judgment starts early in all of us?

"Judge not, that you be not judged," Jesus said in Matthew 7:1. You don't want to be judged, right? We have no idea what is going on with each mom every day, what she's been through, even that day . . . Let's choose to extend more grace to them than judgment. Each of us is doing what we can. Give grace to others, Mama—and remember the grace you have received from the Lord!

Mama, we live in a fallen, judgmental world. I myself have been guilty of judging others, but these passages from Scripture are great reminders in how to rethink our judgmental attitudes. If we judge another mom—or even ourselves!—we are judging another person whom God has fearfully and wonderfully made. Do not look down on His works, but instead let God be the ultimate Judge. Today, let's end with some truth from James 4:12: "There is only one lawgiver and judge, he who is able to save and to destroy. But who are you to judge your neighbor?"

The Mirror

So we have come to know and
to believe the love that God has for us.
God is love, and whoever abides in love
abides in God, and God abides in him.

1 JOHN 4:16

Mama, picture your children. Think about how much love you have for them and how you try to guide them on the right path . . . love them no matter what . . . are there for them in good times and in bad . . . and want them to come to you when they need an ear to listen or a loving embrace.

What's so beautiful is that just as we love our kids so much and do all these things for them, God loves us too—He wants to do the same for you, Mama. Your own mothering instincts are really a mirror of God's own love, and it's such a great reminder of how He sees you and cares for you—just as you do your own children. He tries to guide you on the right path to live out His plans for your life; He loves you no matter what (we're all sinners!); He's always there for you and stays with you—in good times and in bad; He's always there to lend an ear and cover you with His never-ending love. We are reminded in 1 John 4 that God is love. His love for each of us is so great that we can't even imagine it.

Just like kids can get mad at their parents, we too can

find ourselves getting angry at God. But when your kids get angry at you, doesn't that hurt you—especially if you were doing something that was in their best interest? Sometimes God will do things we don't necessarily like, but it's for our best interest. He sees you, Mama, and all the hard, good work you're putting in each day for your children, so don't feel like it goes unseen. Through Him, you can carry on each day, finding rest and strength through Him. Always remember, Mama, that God is for you, and He loves you *so very much!*

Mama, when it's hard to see God's love for you, return to the words of this devotion. Be reminded that just as you try to do your best for your children, God does what's best for you. It's like a mirror of sorts, and as you look into that mirror, you will see God's love reflecting off it. You will be able to see that just as you're doing good things for your children, He's doing them for you too. Just as you'll never stop loving your children, He'll never stop loving you. He will always be there for you—and your children—forever.

Your Children Are Worthy

So God created man in his own image,
in the image of God he created him;
male and female he created them.

GENESIS 1:27

In the kitchen last night, I spotted a ring in its box that my four-year-old daughter had received as a gift when she was born. It's usually in her jewelry box, so I thought maybe she had taken it out to play with it that day. It wasn't until I put her to bed that night that I got the real story as to why she had pulled out the ring. She told me, "Mommy, I asked a boy to marry me today. He said no. I wanted to cry." I felt so bad for my little girl, and I reminded her that God was preparing a husband just for her someday and that she was a beautiful little girl. I told her God had made her so wonderfully and that she was worthy of the very best husband ever!

Rejection and sadness can start so early in our lives, and as kids get older, it happens more and more often. But we can't allow these situations to determine our children's worth; Mama, help them to know this is just a part of life— and that God always has something better planned! Even though you can't get married at the age of four, I know this is something my daughter dreams of someday—just as I did. (I shared with her that I didn't meet her daddy until I was twenty-five, and there would be plenty of boys who would come into her life before God had "the one" ready for her.) I love these conversations with my kids—I hope you are having them with your children too! Mama, help them to know their worth so when someone upsets them it doesn't crush their soul, or so they don't base their worth on what others say about them—no matter what age they are.

Mama, your child is so worthy! Help your kids to know this truth and even use times of trials or rejection to remind them that it doesn't lessen or change their worth—they are already worthy of love and grace and amazing blessings. God's plans are always better, even when we can't see it. Things won't happen if they're not supposed to, and God puts roadblocks on any path He doesn't want us to go down. Rejection is a part of life, but we can choose to look at the positive and keep our eyes focused on God. He's the One who brings us joy!

Put It in Perspective

And we know that for those who love God
all things work together for good,
for those who are called according to his purpose.

ROMANS 8:28

Mama, how many times do you sigh in frustration when your child doesn't do what you've asked them to? During those times, it's important to keep things in perspective. Instead of getting so upset about the little things, replace them with truth. Is their bed not made? They do have a bed to sleep in—and that's a blessing. Did your daughter do an art project that left a mess of glitter everywhere? She was being creative—and that's a blessing. Did your toddler not pick up his toys? He's experienced joy today by playing with toys—and that's a blessing. Did you argue with your teenager about who's taking the car? At least you have a car—and that's a blessing! Looking for the positive in a situation doesn't discount the moment, and yes, they should do the things you have asked them to do, but instead of getting upset and letting the enemy win, stay focused on the bigger picture that God has blessed you and allowed you to provide for your children.

Mama, kids grow up sooner than we think. We can either

put things into perspective or let each situation bother us. Mama, just as you strive to give others grace, you have to learn to extend grace to your kids. As they see you extend grace—they will learn to do so as well. Isn't being like Jesus and extending grace what we want to teach them in the long run anyway?

 Mama, you can choose not to let the little things ruin your day, but instead find ways to replace your negative thoughts with blessings and ways to guide our children and even be blessings to them. No matter what, Mama, they look up to you, and if all they hear is negativity from you, they're going to be worn down, just like you probably feel. Balance is key, and putting things into perspective is so important. Mama, you may feel the pain and stress, but never forget, you were made for this!

The Perfect Mom

For all have sinned and fall short
of the glory of God.
ROMANS 3:23

We all have a mental picture of the perfect mom. In your mind, what does she look like? What does she do that makes her seem so perfect? If you start comparing yourself to "her," you will likely feel like you come up short. But, Mama, I'm here to tell you that God didn't choose "her" to be your children's mom—He chose *you*!

You are the perfect mom for your children, and the glorified, imaginary version of the "perfect mom" isn't. It can be difficult when you go on social media and see other houses perfectly clean or another mom who has time to do all the things as well as get a perfect dinner on the table perfectly, and that can tear you down inside. That prompts me to say this: If there is anyone whom you follow on social media or read about that brings you down inside rather than builds you up, unfollow. Unfollow them now. It does more damage than good when you compare yourself to something online that isn't even realistic.

Let's face it: Social media and the internet show just snippets of real life, perfected photos that have been planned out and perfected—many times through a filter! I much prefer the "real" photos—the pots and pans in the sink that resulted in the home-cooked meal that was made with love!

In what areas do you feel like you're falling short as you compare yourself to other moms online or in real life? Is this even something that would make you feel better and more complete if you could improve in that area? You don't have to obtain perfection, but sometimes working on a certain area can make us feel more positive in life. And, Mama, there's certainly a gift you have that you can use to help another mom with who is struggling. Maybe you make the best banana bread, and you know another mom who can't bake for anything—you might exchange tips and help one another out. That would be a great way to give back while learning something new!

Canceled Plans

"Come to me,
all who labor and are heavy laden,
and I will give you rest."

MATTHEW 11:28

Holidays and parties can be a lot of fun, especially when we get to see our family and friends and we hope to enjoy a great time. But being a busy mom means that even parties (especially when keeping track of kiddos) aren't always as fun as we might have thought. We put a lot of pressure on ourselves when it comes to hosting too—to make sure the house is clean, we have enough food on hand, and everyone has a good time. Sometimes canceled plans can be an answer to prayer! Just spending Christmas without any expectations and only with our families can bring us the rest we really need. Staying in your PJ's all day with the kids with cinnamon rolls baking in the oven? Yes, please!

Sometimes all the running around, with all the high expectations, can prevent us from getting the rest we really need, especially during the holidays. Don't forget: Memories can be made even in the simplest of times. Not everything needs to be extravagant, nor do you necessarily have to drive to three different houses just to make everyone happy on

Christmas Day. Sometimes the simplest of times create the best memories.

Think of it in the opposite way too. If a family member or friend cancels on you and your holiday dinner, don't fret or judge, but instead, extend grace. They might just need some rest too, and that may be the only time they can have with their own immediate family—that's okay! Canceled plans—they aren't the end of the world. Mama, always keep the big picture in mind!

 *Mama, take the pressure off yourself in trying to please everyone! That's a hard job, and as we learned, we should be more concerned about pleasing the Lord. When holidays become more of a burden than what they are worth, take a step back and ask yourself whether it's worth all the stress. It's okay to say no to parties and find rest in just staying home with your family now and then. Keeping it simple can make some of the very best memories.*

Humble and Kind

But he gives more grace.
Therefore it says, "God opposes the proud
but gives grace to the humble."

JAMES 4:6

What does success look like to you? For some people, it means working up the corporate ladder or making lots of money. But worldly success doesn't always equal happiness. Having money doesn't either. As we work hard each day, we need to look at our success and whom we give the credit to. We need to push down our pride and the "look what I did" attitude to instead give God the glory and keep ourselves humble.

No matter how big or small our successes may be, we should always honor the One who gets us there. This is something to also instill in our children—to stay humble and kind. When they achieve success by winning the basketball championship or having their artwork place at the show, help them to stay humble, thankful to God, and kind to others. The wins we achieve in life don't make us better than other people. And we shouldn't try to make others feel bad when they didn't win the race, game, show, or whatever else.

As we work to instill a humble attitude in our children, let them catch you being this way too. I remember growing up and watching my dad being humble and kind to others. It wasn't until I was older that I learned he had worked his way up at his company as an engineer to end his career in a high position there. He was always humble about his successes in life, and he never made anyone feel bad or think he was any better than they were. I am now sharing the same lessons with my own kids—just as you should too, Mama!

Mama, it's so fun to watch our kids win at sports and other activities, and it's great to even have those wins and success in our own lives too! But in the end, we must always stay humble and kind. Instead of boasting or being proud in front of other people, we should give credit to the One who has enabled us or our children's successes. First Peter 5:6 gives us a great reminder: "Humble yourselves, therefore, under the mighty hand of God so that at the proper time he may exalt you."

at the right time I, the Lord will make it happen.

ISAIAH 60:22 NLT

Roots

Jesus said to her, "Everyone who drinks of this water will be thirsty again, but whoever drinks of the water that I will give him will never be thirsty again. The water that I will give him will become in him a spring of water welling up to eternal life."

JOHN 4:13-14

Have you ever transplanted a plant into new soil? I did this recently with a few plants, and well, they got shocked and did not do well in their new environment. People are much the same way. We can plant our roots, deep into the soil we're used to, but when change happens, we can go into shock, just like our plants.

I experienced some life changes recently, and when some of my own roots were pulled up, I got shocked. When you switch homes . . . or jobs . . . or churches . . . it can come as a shock. It can be a challenge for our roots to settle in and feel comfortable in the new soil. But do you know what really helps plants to adjust to their new surroundings? Water. When we abundantly water our plants when they are planted in new soil, they will "take" better as the soil gets wet around the roots. The same is true for people: As we enter new seasons of life, we need to be watered by the Spirit. We need to be in prayer and focusing on the Lord rather than the discomfort of the new spot we're in. We can come to the Living Water and let the soil around us be watered so that the transition is easier. As we focus on His plans for us, rather than our own, the adjustment will be a bit smoother.

Don't get me wrong—change is not always easy. But as we allow our roots to take hold in new soil, we can grow stronger in our faith and God's calling for our lives. And as our roots grow stronger and deeper, when storms come (as they always do), we can stay grounded in our faith in Him. When drought comes and the soil becomes dry, run to the Lord for an extra drink of water from the well, and let Him quench your soul thirst—because He will.

Mama, the story of the woman at the well from John 4 demonstrates that Jesus is the Living Water. Water is a symbol of salvation and relationship with God, Jesus, and the Holy Spirit. Just like both plants and people need water physically to thrive, we also need the Living Water to secure our salvation, grounding our roots deep so we can't be shaken. The next time you're in a season of change or a drought, come to the well and take a nice, long drink of the Living Water.

Just Like Us

*But Jesus said, "Let the little children
come to me and do not hinder them,
for to such belongs the kingdom of heaven."*

MATTHEW 19:14

Sometimes, Mama, we can look past an important truth that's right in front of us. One such truth? Our children are only human; they will never be perfect—only Jesus is. They are just like us—little humans who make mistakes, get tired and cranky, become anxious or sad, experience joy and excitement—along with all the other ways we act as humans. They can't read our minds, just as we can't read theirs. Sometimes they need space, and sometimes they need you to be close. They may get upset, or they may be joyful. They get scared, just as we do—and even more so, just as we did when we were younger. We need to look at them through this lens, that they are humans, experiencing human thoughts, emotions, and the need for a Savior. We may not understand why they do the things they do, but we *can* understand that they are human beings.

Matthew 19 is a great reminder that Jesus loves children, for the kingdom of heaven belongs to them. Each of us can come to Jesus at any time, for anything, anywhere. Mama, today try to place yourself in the shoes of your children, asking the Lord to help you better understand where they're coming from. We may not understand them fully, but the Lord knows each of us more than we even know ourselves . . . and He can see what's up ahead when we can't. Trust in Him—He loves the little children!

 *Take heart, Mama, and give both yourself and your kids some grace. Remind yourself that they are just little (or big) humans, so you can give them grace as you realize they have human tendencies (just like you), and they won't ever be perfect. We all experience the same emotions—we can be upset or frustrated or sad—but it's all a part of the human experience. Enter grace for them—and for yourself too. In difficult moments, try to remember what it was like when you were their age. We are all different and unique, and we respond to situations differently. Each child is different too. But, Mama, God chose you to be their mom—you were made for this!*

Forgiving

Be kind to one another,
tenderhearted, forgiving one another,
as God in Christ forgave you.
EPHESIANS 4:32

Do you find it easy or hard to forgive when someone hurts or offends you? Have you ever felt the weight of holding on to a grievance for too long? It's easy at times to take hurtful situations to heart, but Mama, why would you want to hold on to the pain? If we can forgive those who have slighted us, and give the situation to God to handle, He will replace the weight of this heavy burden with the joy that is only found in Jesus.

In John 16:33, Jesus reminds us of this: "I have said these things to you, that in me you may have peace. In the world you will have tribulation. But take heart; I have overcome the world." In Mark 11:25, Jesus also instructs us this way: "And whenever you stand praying, forgive, if you have anything against anyone, so that your Father also who is in heaven may forgive you your trespasses."

Mama, don't you want to be forgiven when you are in the wrong? Let's demonstrate to our children what it looks like to forgive and encourage them to do the same. Most people like to hold on to grudges and feel hurt when an offender doesn't "get what they deserve," but we are called to be different! And besides, God is the ultimate Judge: "For we must all appear before the judgment seat of Christ, so that each one may receive what is due for what he has done in the body, whether good or evil" (II Corinthians 5:10).

Mama, let's be the forgiving people the Lord has called us to be—it will be a weight off your shoulders and bring you a healthy dose of God's peace.

Mama, whom do you need to forgive today? What's holding you back from doing so? Today, Mama, release what you've been holding on to—no matter how big or how small—to Jesus. With an honest heart, pour your hurt out to the Lord and release those who need to receive your forgiveness today. As you forgive others, you should also teach your children to do the same, so they can feel the release, the joy, and the peace that come from a heart that freely forgives.

Cleaning House

"Do not store up for yourselves treasures on earth,
where moths and vermin destroy,
and where thieves break in and steal.
But store up for yourselves treasures in heaven,
where moths and vermin do not destroy,
and where thieves do not break in and steal.
For where your treasure is,
there your heart will be also."

MATTHEW 6:19–21 NIV

Mama, doesn't a clean house feel good? I know I feel so much better when I'm not stepping on Cheerios and when all things are in their place. During our last home renovation, I decided it was time to get rid of things that no longer served our family, to live a little more simply with just what we needed. This has made my home filled with less— and now there is less to clean up, and we live in a little more peace. Not only that, but we were able to give to those who needed those things we had but didn't use. They were just sitting collecting dust and taking up valuable space.

Mama, not only is it good to clean the clutter out of our homes, but it's also good to clean out our minds, hearts, and souls. Take a look at what's causing all the clutter—what is buried in an old box deep inside that you need to get rid of by giving it to God? What is no longer serving you that you need to release to the Lord? This could include emotions or offenses that are weighing you down, preventing you from living more freely.

When we start to get rid of things that no longer serve us—both in our homes and in our souls—it becomes so much easier to clean house. Of course, each week things get dirty again, and a new housecleaning needs to happen, but if we keep clearing out the clutter, oh, how much more freedom we'll experience!

Mama, don't let stuff fester . . . and don't give earthly things more value than they really have. We are to store our treasures in heaven rather than on this earth. God gives and He takes away, for our things aren't really ours, they're His. "Yet for us there is one God, the Father, from whom are all things and for whom we exist, and one Lord, Jesus Christ, through whom are all things and through whom we exist" (1 Corinthians 8:6).

He Will Provide

"Therefore do not be anxious, saying,
'What shall we eat?' or 'What shall we drink?'
or 'What shall we wear?'
For the Gentiles seek after all these things,
and your heavenly Father knows
that you need them all."

MATTHEW 6:31–32

Mama, it is a lot of responsibility to be a mother. We moms do all we can for our families, and we can sometimes wonder if God will provide for what's next—whether that's a new job, the high price of food at the grocery store, or a new home that can accommodate a growing family. Our worries may seem endless, but God *does* provide for us—endlessly. He knows your heart, Mama, and He knows what your family needs. He is working in and through the circumstances of your lives, sometimes years ahead of time, and even as you sleep, He never stops working for you!

Jesus gave us such a great reminder in Luke 12:24: "Consider the ravens: they neither sow nor reap, they have neither storehouse nor barn, and yet God feeds them. Of how much more value are you than the birds!" Mama, you and your family have far more value than the birds. There may be times when God provides for us in ways we don't understand or that we may be afraid to accept. But know this, that even when we can't see why or how, God does . . . so be patient and keep saying yes to the calling and provisions He places before you. Run, even blindly if need be, toward Him, and keep your eyes focused on His plans. Seek Him and pray. God knows what you need, and He will provide for you—always.

With God providing for you and your family, Mama, you can leave your worries in His hands. Have you ever been in a season of needing provision—or are you in it now? When you look back over your life, can you see how God provided when you needed it most? Even as you made important decisions about your career, or your education, or where to live, or whom to marry . . . Mama, God was in it all, and He still is. So take a deep breath, exhaling doubt and inhaling trust that He will always give you just what you need.

Generation to Generation

The way of a fool is right in his own eyes,
but a wise man listens to advice.

PROVERBS 12:15

Do you remember how, when you first became a mom, everyone seemed to have "advice" for you? Sometimes that advice went against new ways of parenting, or it made you question whether you were doing the right thing as a mom. Sometimes what worked for our parents and grandparents doesn't work for us today. Things change, and rules change, and what was safe or good in our grandmothers' time may not be the same for us. But we can also learn from the timeless knowledge and wisdom they pass down to us, so don't be so quick to dismiss their advice either.

As you receive parenting advice from others, consider what you've heard, reflect on whether it aligns with your values and parenting style, and choose to incorporate what feels right for your family.

And if you choose not to take the advice you've been given, don't feel guilty. (Even the advice I give in this book may not work for every family—and that's okay too!) But there is some advice we *should* all listen to—and that is the godly counsel we receive from the Word of God. Proverbs 19:27

tells us: "Cease to hear instruction . . . and you will stray from the words of knowledge." At the end of the day, you can always count on God's advise. Ask God to guide you as you make decisions. Ask Him to help you decide what advise to take and what advise to dismiss. If you follow His steps, you won't be led astray.

Mama, you were made to be your child's mother. God put you in charge of raising your child, and you will know best what's right for your little (or big) one, more than the world could ever know. Yes, times will change from generation to generation, and someday you'll be a grandma too, offering advice to your own progeny. You'll need to remember this then too—that not all advice will be taken, but it can be taken into consideration. Moms know their children well—but God knows them inside and out. So seek Him, and let Him be your greatest advice giver.

You Are Loved

We love because he first loved us.

I JOHN 4:19

Mama, *you are loved!* This verse from I John is one of my favorites because it reminds me of why we love others: It's because of His great love for us! "So we have come to know and to believe the love that God has for us. God is love, and whoever abides in love abides in God, and God abides in him" (I John 4:16).

In your role as a mother, you may not get as many thank-yous as you deserve or get the full rest you need, Mama, but you are showing love in all you do for your family. Don't let that go without saying or without notice, because God notices it—and your family does too. They love you beyond measure.

A mother's love is never given in order to receive praise, but rather, she pours it out of her heart and her soul. I know at the end of the day, I'm exhausted, and you likely are too, but Mama, think of all the mothers before us who have done it all too (and they had to wash clothes by hand!). It wasn't until I became a mom myself that I realized how much love a mother has for her children. Wouldn't you agree? You likely see your own parents in a new light now that you are a parent yourself. They sacrificed, they shopped, they planned, and they gave their time, love, and attention—all to raise . . . you! Now it's our turn to give that same love and devotion to our children.

Mama, there will be a day when the house is quiet and the dirty diaper pail no longer exists . . . so soak up each day, no matter what season you're in with your kids! There will come a day when they're off on their own (or they may be already!), and you will know, Mama, that all the time and energy you invested in their lives is all worth it. Thank you, Mama, for all you do and continue to do, for a mother's job is never done!

You mirror God's love in so many different ways, and Mama, you exude it every single day. You are love to your children, just as your heavenly Father is love to you. You are the safe haven for your kids, their support, their warmth. Yes, motherhood can be draining, but that's because you're pouring it all out day after day. Mama, as I John tells us, you love because God loves you— never forget that. You are doing a beautiful and amazing thing by being a mom—and you were made for this!

Building Trust

Trust in the LORD with all your heart,
and do not lean on your own understanding.

PROVERBS 3:5

Mama, do you trust the Lord with all your heart? If you had any bit of doubt in your soul when you read that question, why is that? Sometimes the enemy can swoop in and whisper in our ear a long list of how "God has failed you," causing doubt to set in. At other times, the Lord tells us to go one way, but we think our way is best and so we travel our own path. As human beings, we sometimes need to be reminded not to lean on our own understanding. We can always come up with reasons not to do something, but take heart, Mama. God sees what we can't . . . He understands what we can't . . . and He has already prepared the path before you. Even when you don't feel equipped or ready, He will make the way straight for you.

Mama, build up your trust and faith in the Lord, rather than fostering doubt and mistrust. As you step forward and start your faith journey with the Lord, it can be hard at first, but as you learn to trust Him with your decisions, even your very life, you can rest in the peace and assurance that your ways don't compare to His. Follow the words of Proverbs 3 and trust in the Lord with all your heart—not just *some* but *all.* When raising your children too, teach them to trust in the Lord. They will not always understand the reasons certain things happen, but you, as their mama, can help build their faith and trust roots. Bring it all back to God, who has something better planned, Do not lean on your earthly understanding, but rather, release it all to Him, and He will work it out for the good of both you and your children.

Do you have a hard time with trust, Mama? We often hold in our minds examples of how we've been hurt in the past and how our trust failed us . . . but who better to trust than the Creator of the universe? He is the Alpha and the Omega. He knows everyone and everything better than our minds could ever fathom. Mama, today you are invited to put your trust in God. You may not understand why or even like the outcomes, but just wait . . . God is good, so keep putting your faith and trust in Him, and teach your children this as well. Build up those faith roots, and keep your eyes on Him!

You Were Made for This!

For you created my inmost being;
you knit me together in my mother's womb. I praise you
because I am fearfully and wonderfully made;
your works are wonderful, I know that full well.

PSALM 139:13–14 NIV

Mama, you have been fearfully and wonderfully made! God has given you a special and a wonderful blessing—to be a mother. No matter how that came to be, you were *chosen*. God loves you, He sees you, and you are such a blessing in the lives of your children and your family!

Mama, you have such beautiful and wonderful gifts, so graciously given to you by our Lord, with which you are privileged to serve your family each and every day. Push away and lift to the Lord any negativity, mom guilt, and anything else that might be stealing joy from your beautiful soul. Although you may not get the thanks you deserve each day, know that you are doing amazing things, Mama, and the work doesn't go unnoticed by the Lord. Being a mom comes with some days full of beautiful memories—and other days filled with stress and trials—but count them all as joy during your motherhood journey. Never forget that God is beside you, each day, and He will guide you through every circumstance. Seek Him in both the peaks and the valleys, and praise Him, even in the storms.

Mama, you are doing a beautiful thing—know that you are worthy! Practice patience and grace daily, especially with yourself. As you view yourself in the mirror, tell the woman looking back at you the beautiful things you see in her. Be deliberate to put down the phone more, and instead look your children in the eye as you tell them how much they mean to you and how much God loves them. Remember, each child is unique, so celebrate the way God made them so perfectly. Help them to discover their God-given gifts. Your children won't always remember what you did, but they'll always remember how you made them feel. Mama, you are doing an incredible job!

Mama, you were made for this! You were specifically made to be a mother to your children. I hope this book has helped you realize that time goes by fast, so you should soak in each moment. We can worry so much about what others think or what we should do, but the better path is to find peace in Jesus. I hope you know that you are a beautiful person and that you are doing great things! Never forget, Mama, that God has placed you in your family as your children's mother, and that is a wonderful blessing. You were made for this!

DaySpring

LIVE YOUR FAITH

Dear Friend,

This book was prayerfully crafted with you, the reader, in mind. Every word, every sentence, every page was thoughtfully written, designed, and packaged to encourage you—right where you are this very moment. At DaySpring, our vision is to see every person experience the life-changing message of God's love. So, as we worked through rough drafts, design changes, edits, and details, we prayed for you to deeply experience His unfailing love, indescribable peace, and pure joy. It is our sincere hope that through these Truth-filled pages your heart will be blessed, knowing that God cares about you—your desires and disappointments, your challenges and dreams.

He knows. He cares. He loves you unconditionally.

BLESSINGS!
THE DAYSPRING BOOK TEAM

Additional copies of this book and
other DaySpring titles can be purchased
at fine retailers everywhere.
Order online at <u>dayspring.com</u>
or
by phone at 1-877-751-4347